KIDS BAKE!

GOOD
HOUSEKEEPING
KIDS BAKE!

100+ SWEET AND SAVORY RECIPES

HEARST
books

CONTENTS

GLAZED CINNAMON
ROLLS • PAGE 107

FOREWORD

After the success of *Kids Cook!*, I'm excited to share our new companion book, *Kids Bake!*

Do you remember the first time you baked something? Dumping flour, scooping cookie dough, and playing with pie dough scraps is how many of us got our first kitchen experiences. And the payoff is still memorable: inhaling the aroma of baking butter and sugar, watching pizza rise and puff through the glass of the oven door, and taking your first bites of a warm chocolate-chip cookie.

Now it's time to pass along the joy of baking to the next generation! To assemble this collection, I got to spend time looking through hundreds of *Good Housekeeping*'s baking recipes. A delicious task! These best-of-the-best recipes are gathered from every baking category. I'm happy to report that, in addition to all the sweet treats you could want, this book goes beyond just desserts. Who would argue with a whole chapter on pizza? And once you try our Granola Bars (page 45) or Glazed Cinnamon Rolls (page 107), you won't want to buy them again!

We've got step-by-step treats, like our Flowerpot Cupcakes (page 58), that will engage even the youngest bakers. Plus, for the more experienced bakers who want to graduate from cookies, we offer a fabulous selection of layer cakes, pies, and yeast doughs.

Whether you're passing the potholders to your tween to start baking solo or looking for a guide of family-friendly recipes to try with your younger child, *Kids Bake!* is full of delicious, easy options in a fun, accessible format. There's everything you'll need to get started, from Smart Chef advice to safety info, equipment options, measuring tips, and much more.

So, ladies and gentlemen, start your ovens! Here's to the next generation of budding bakers!

SUSAN WESTMORELAND
Food Director, *Good Housekeeping*

READY, SET, BAKE!

Congratulations! You picked up *Good Housekeeping Kids Bake!*, which means you're already on your way to baking something amazing. We've got a world of treats for you to try—from yummy cookies, cakes, and pies to fabulous muffins, breads, and pizzas. Baking involves a bit of science and some funny-sounding techniques, but don't let those details scare you away from experiencing fresh-out-of-the-oven deliciousness! Once you've learned a few simple basics from this book, baking will come more naturally and will start to be a lot of fun. So let's begin!

1. **READ** the recipe from start to finish (ask an adult if you have any questions). Make sure you have enough time to make the recipe without having to rush.

2. **GATHER** all the ingredients, equipment, and tools that you'll need.

3. **PLACE** the oven rack(s) in the correct position(s) before turning on the oven. Most of our recipes use the center oven rack (unless specified otherwise).

4. **PREHEAT** the oven at least 15 minutes before you put anything in it.

5. **PREPARE** your baking pan(s) as the recipe directs.

6. **MEASURE** out all the ingredients before you start mixing.

7. **POSITION** a single pan in the center of the oven rack for proper air circulation. Place multiple pans in the oven so they don't touch each other or the oven sides.

8. **SET** the timer once your project is in the oven.

9. **KEEP** clean, dry oven mitts or pads nearby.

10. **GET** your cooling racks ready.

EQUIPMENT & TOOLS

Recipes in this book require some basic equipment, plus some items you'll find in every baker's tool kit. No need to have every tool on this list. You can collect more tools as you gain baking confidence and try more recipes.

ELECTRIC MIXER A heavy-duty, stand-mounted machine, with its powerful motor, can handle everything from delicate cake batter to stiff cookie dough. Stand mixers come with an assortment of bowls and attachments for several mixing chores. For small jobs, like whipping cream, use a handheld mixer.

FOOD PROCESSOR For chopping, grating, kneading, and mixing in a flash.

BAKING PANS Metal pans with sides 1½ to 2 inches high. Choose pans made from aluminum or heavy tin-plated steel. Essential are 8 x 8–inch and 9 x 9–inch square pans and a 13 x 9–inch rectangular pan. Note: Baking dishes are usually made of ovenproof glass or ceramic. Glass generates a higher amount of heat than metal, so only use if specified in a recipe.

COOKIE SHEETS Flat metal sheets with slightly raised edges on one or more sides. Have several on hand for baking cookies (they should cool down before you reuse them) and for placing under pies, which may leak during baking. Cookie sheets should fit in your oven with 2 inches to spare on all sides.

COOLING RACKS Use round wire racks for cake layers and rectangular wire racks for cookies and larger baked goods.

LAYER CAKE PANS Medium-weight aluminum pans are best. Have three 8-inch and three 9-inch round cake pans that are at least 1½ inches deep.

RIMMED BAKING SHEET A rectangular metal pan with low sides (15½ x 10½ inches is the standard size).

PIE PLATES Made of ovenproof glass, metal, or ceramic. Our recipes call for a 9-inch pie plate. Avoid disposable foil pans, as they hold less than standard pie plates and tend to be flimsy.

TUBE PAN A deep metal cake pan with a tube in the middle that gives the batter a surface to stick to as it rises. A tube pan comes in one piece or with a removable bottom.

GRATER The most versatile is a box grater with different-size holes on each side for grating chocolate or shredding cheese.

PASTRY BAG AND ASSORTED TIPS For decorating cakes, cupcakes, and cookies. Tips can be round or star-shaped.

ROLLING PIN For evenly rolling out dough for pies, tarts, and cookies. Choose an American-style, hardwood, free-spinning pin with a ball bearing for the most control.

SPATULAS A variety of spatulas in different sizes is a must for baking. *Rubber spatulas* are used to fold in flour mixtures as well as to scrape bowls. A *wide metal spatula* is used to remove cookies and pizzas from hot cookie sheets. A *narrow metal spatula* or *mini offset spatula* is the go-to tool for frosting cakes and cupcakes and spreading glazes.

BASIC INGREDIENTS

Be sure to have frequently used ingredients like butter, chocolate chips, and vanilla extract on hand. Most basic ingredients keep well in the pantry, fridge, or freezer. Having a healthy stock of them in your kitchen makes it easier for you to whip up a recipe at a moment's notice. You just never know when those cravings will call!

BAKING POWDER This leavening is highly perishable, so keep it in a cool, dry place with the container tightly closed. Discard any baking powder you've had longer than a year.

BAKING SODA Always mix this leavening with the other dry ingredients before any liquid is added. Once the dry and liquid ingredients are combined, place the batter in the oven quickly.

BUTTER It brings out a rich, sweet taste in baked goods that nothing else can match. Our recipes use salted butter unless specified otherwise.

BUTTERMILK Use only when specified; it balances sugar's sweetness and reacts with baking soda to give baked goods a fine, crumbly texture.

CHOCOLATE *Unsweetened chocolate* contains 50–58 percent cocoa butter and no sugar. Do not substitute unsweetened chocolate with semisweet. *Semisweet chocolate* can be used interchangeably with *bittersweet chocolate,* but semisweet chocolate has more sugar, which results in a less intense flavor.

EGGS Our recipes call for large eggs.

EXTRACTS Use pure, not imitation, extracts whenever possible to obtain the truest flavor. Vanilla is most commonly used, but several of our recipes call for almond extract.

FLOUR All recipes for this book call for all-purpose flour. Although bleached and unbleached can be used interchangeably, we prefer bleached flour for cakes and pies because it produces a more tender and delicate result.

MILK Use plain whole milk to achieve the desired richness in baked goods, or substitute low-fat (2 percent) milk.

NUTS AND SEEDS Their high fat content makes them perishable. Buy shelled, not chopped, nuts in airtight containers. Store nuts and seeds in zip-close plastic bags in the freezer. To toast nuts, spread in a single layer on a rimmed baking sheet and bake at 350°F for about 10 minutes or until lightly browned and fragrant, stirring occasionally.

OIL We recommend using a flavorless vegetable oil for baking, such as corn, safflower, or canola. Do not substitute oil for solid shortening in any baking recipe.

SALT Without salt, sweet baked goods may taste flat. Use table salt for recipes in this book unless otherwise specified.

SPICES Keep in a cool, dark place—away from heat and moisture.

SUGAR More than a sweetener, sugar helps batters and doughs rise by allowing more air to be incorporated as the mixture is beaten. It also keeps cakes and cookies tender and moist.

UNSWEETENED COCOA is a powder made by removing most of the fat from chocolate. Do not substitute instant cocoa mix, as it contains sugar.

> **SMART CHEF!** Check the freshness dates on any ingredients that have them before you start to bake.

Measure with Accuracy

Our recipes depend on the correct *ratio* of ingredients (the amount of one ingredient in relation to another)—plus chemistry—to work. But you don't have to be a scientist to bake like a pro. Just follow these simple rules:

USE THE RIGHT MEASURES—metal or plastic measuring cups for dry ingredients, and glass or clear plastic measuring cups with spouts for liquids.

SPOON DRY INGREDIENTS (like flour, cornmeal, unsweetened cocoa, and sugar) into the dry measuring cup until it is overflowing. Before measuring flour, loosen it with a fork or spoon in the bag or container. Do not pack flour down or tap the measuring cup. Level off the excess flour with a straightedge (like the back of a knife or a metal spatula).

FIRMLY PACK BROWN SUGAR into a dry measuring cup and level it off. It should hold its shape when turned out of the cup.

PLACE YOUR LIQUID MEASURING CUP on the countertop. Make sure your eyes are at the same level as the measuring marks. Pour the liquid into the cup until it's right at the mark—not above or below. For sticky ingredients (like maple syrup, honey, and molasses) spray the measuring cup with nonstick cooking spray before measuring for easy cleaning later.

USE MEASURING SPOONS, not eating utensils, to measure small amounts. For dry ingredients, scoop the measuring spoon into the container until the ingredient is overflowing, then level it off. For liquid ingredients, pour liquid until it reaches the top edge of the spoon. Measure over a separate cup or bowl so any extra liquid does not fall into your batter or dough.

Equivalent Measurements

This convenient chart helps you measure with accuracy.

THIS MUCH...	IS THE SAME AS...
pinch	the amount you can pick up between your thumb and forefinger
dash	less than ⅛ teaspoon
1½ teaspoons	½ tablespoon
3 teaspoons	1 tablespoon
1 cup	½ pint
2 cups	1 pint
4 cups (2 pints)	1 quart
¼ pound	4 ounces
½ pound	8 ounces
¾ pound	12 ounces
1 pound	16 ounces
4 tablespoons	¼ cup
5 tablespoons plus 1 teaspoon	⅓ cup
8 tablespoons	½ cup
10 tablespoons plus 2 teaspoons	⅔ cup
16 tablespoons	1 cup

Nutrition by Numbers

Food naturally contains nutrients—like protein, fat, and carbohydrates—that provide energy. Some nutrients, like fiber and sodium, don't provide energy but are also important for health. Your body needs the right combination of nutrients to work properly and grow. We've included the per-serving amount of each of these nutrients in every recipe so you know what you're eating.

Here are some terms to help you read nutritional information:

Nutrients are weighed in grams (g) and milligrams (mg). One teaspoon of water weighs 5 grams; one teaspoon of sugar weighs about 4 grams.

CALORIES tell you the total amount of energy in your food and can come from fat, protein, or carbohydrates. The amount of calories you need per day depends on your age, size, and activity level.

PROTEIN helps your body build and repair muscles, blood, and organs. High-protein foods include meat, poultry, fish, eggs, beans, lentils, nuts, and seeds.

FAT is an important nutrient that your body uses for growth and development. However, not all fats are the same. *Healthy fats* include vegetable and nut oils, which provide essential fatty acids and vitamin E. Healthy fat is also naturally found in avocados and seafood. On the other hand, *saturated fat*, which comes from animal sources like red meat, poultry, and full-fat dairy products, should be limited.

CARBOHYDRATES are your body's primary source of energy. You'll find *simple carbohydrates* in fruits, vegetables, and milk, as well as some sugars. *Complex carbohydrates* include whole-grain breads and cereals, starchy vegetables, and legumes (think beans and peanuts). Most complex carbs contain *fiber*, which makes you feel full and aids digestion.

SODIUM (translation: salt) is used by our bodies to conduct nerve impulses, contract and relax muscles, and stay hydrated—but you only need it in small amounts. Too much sodium in your diet can lead to high blood pressure, heart disease, and stroke.

Baking Pans 101

Practically all our recipes use a baking pan, so let's get familiar with these basics:

PICK YOUR PAN. Use the pan size called for in a recipe. This will keep your dough or batter from burning or overflowing during baking. To check the size, use a ruler to measure across the top of the pan, from inside edge to inside edge. Measure the depth on the inside as well, from the bottom to the top of the pan.

KNOW YOUR PAN. Shiny metal and dark metal pans cook differently. Shiny pans are best for cakes because they reflect heat away from the cake and produce a tender, light-brown crust. Dark and nonstick pans absorb more heat, so if you're using one of them, reduce the oven temperature in the recipe by 25°F. (Same goes for glass baking dishes.)

PREP YOUR PAN. Grease and flour a pan if directed in a recipe. Rub a piece of butter or vegetable shortening all over the inside of the pan to make a thin coating. Working over the sink, sprinkle some flour into the pan. Shake and tilt the pan until it is coated. Turn the pan upside down and tap out the excess flour.

Baker's Lingo

Baking has many terms for different methods and techniques. This collection of short definitions will help you decode our recipes.

BAKE To cook with dry, radiant heat in an oven.

BATTER A mixture of flour, eggs, dairy, or other ingredients that create a pourable liquid.

BEAT To stir very rapidly with a spoon, whisk, or electric mixer to incorporate air.

BLEND To stir ingredients together until well mixed.

COMBINE To stir ingredients together until just mixed.

CREAM To beat sugar and butter until a light, creamy texture and color have been achieved. This method adds air to batter, which helps the baked good rise. Sometimes eggs are also added during the creaming step.

CRIMP To press together the side and top crusts of a pie in a pretty pattern, using a fork or clean fingers. Crimping helps the dough grip the lip of a pie plate so the filling doesn't seep over the edge during baking.

DRIZZLE To pour a thin stream of a liquid on top of a dish.

DUST To coat the surface of something with a light sprinkling of a dry ingredient (such as flour, sugar, or cocoa powder).

FOLD To gently combine a light, airy ingredient (such as beaten egg whites) with a heavier one (such as cake mix) to create a light, fluffy consistency.

GLAZE To coat with a sugar-based sauce or melted chocolate.

HULL To remove the tough, leafy stem of fruits or nuts before using. To hull berries, insert a plastic straw through the bottom center of each fruit, then push out the green stem.

KNEAD To combine dough by hand on a work surface. This involves folding the dough over, pressing down, turning 90 degrees, and then repeating the process. Kneading mixes the dough and creates gluten strands that give strength to breads and other baked goods.

PIPE To decoratively add frosting (or whipped cream) to a dessert by pressing the mixture through a bag fitted with a fluted tip.

SIFT To put powdery ingredients (like flour or cocoa) through a fine metal sieve to remove any lumps.

SOFTEN To bring butter, cream cheese, or other solid fat to room temperature to make it softer and easier to work with.

SOFT PEAKS To beat egg whites or heavy cream with an electric mixer until a peak bends or slumps over to one side when beaters are lifted.

STIFF PEAKS To beat egg whites or heavy cream with an electric mixer until peaks stand completely straight up when beaters are lifted.

WHISK To stir briskly with a whisk to incorporate air.

Baking Safely

Home-baking is a blast, but it's important to be safe in the kitchen while having fun. Our useful tips will keep you safe from start to finish.

BEFORE YOU BAKE

- **TIE** back long hair.
- **ROLL** up your sleeves and put on a clean apron.
- **CLEAR** off and clean a space big enough to work in.
- **WASH** your hands with warm soapy water before you touch any food.
- **BE CAREFUL** with sharp knives and tools.

WHILE IT BAKES

- **STAY** in the kitchen while the oven is on.
- **PLACE** cooling racks on a clean counter away from where the batter or dough was mixed.
- **WASH** counters, appliance surfaces, and tools in warm soapy water.
- **LISTEN** for the timer to go off.

AS YOU MIX

- **CRACK** eggs in a separate small bowl to avoid broken eggshell in the batter.
- **KEEP** bowls and utensils used for eggs or mixing raw batter or dough separate from dry ingredients and dry measuring tools.
- **PREP** nuts, fruits, or veggies on a clean cutting board.

AFTER IT BAKES

- **USE** dry oven mitts or pads to handle hot pans (wet ones will burn you).
- **REWASH** your hands before handling cooled baked items.

Now that you know the basics, are you ready to get started?

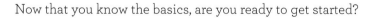

LET'S BAKE!

1

Cookies, Brownies & Bars

Start your baking journey by creating a batch of amazing treats that will make you the talk of the bake sale. We've got cookies of all sorts—from giant Pumpkin-Cherry Breakfast Cookies to Double Chocolate Chip Cookies—and loads of recipes for brownies (some even begin with a mix, to give you a running start) and bars. Are you ready to have a sweet time in the kitchen?

Pumpkin-Cherry
BREAKFAST COOKIES

Cookies for breakfast? Absolutely! Especially when they're made with healthful goodies like oats, pumpkin, and dried cherries.

ACTIVE TIME → 15 MINUTES **TOTAL TIME → 35 MINUTES (PLUS COOLING)** **MAKES → 16 COOKIES**

INGREDIENTS

2 cups whole wheat flour

1 cup old-fashioned oats, uncooked

1 teaspoon baking soda

1 teaspoon pumpkin pie spice

¼ teaspoon salt

1 (15-ounce) can pure pumpkin

1 cup coconut oil

1 cup packed brown sugar

1 large egg

½ cup roasted, salted pepitas (pumpkin seeds)

½ cup dried cherries

EACH COOKIE

Calories: About 290
Protein: 5G
Carbohydrates: 33G
Total Fat: 17G
(Saturated Fat: 12G)
Fiber: 5G
Sodium: 135MG

1. Preheat oven to 350°F. Line large cookie sheet with parchment paper.

2. In large bowl with wire whisk, mix flour, oats, baking soda, pumpkin pie spice, and salt. In large bowl with mixer on medium speed, beat pumpkin, oil, sugar, and egg until well combined. Gradually beat in flour mixture just until combined. Stir in pepitas and cherries.

3. Scoop dough onto prepared cookie sheet to form 16 mounds, 2 inches apart; flatten into disks. Bake for 20 to 25 minutes or until dark brown on bottoms. With metal spatula, transfer cookies to wire racks and let cool completely. Cookies can be made ahead, wrapped in plastic wrap, and stored at room temperature for up to 2 days or frozen for up to 2 weeks. Reheat in a toaster oven until crisp.

WHAT IS IT?

COCONUT OIL is a solid fat made from the inner white flesh of coconuts. Look for coconut oil labeled "unrefined" or "virgin" for a more pronounced tropical taste.

FUN FOOD!

Mini "BLACK & WHITE" COOKIES

We added color to give these classic cookies a bold new look—and we made them into adorable minis! Bake a batch for your next slumber party, where they are sure to be a hit.

ACTIVE TIME → 30 MINUTES   **TOTAL TIME → 1 HOUR** (PLUS COOLING AND STANDING)   **MAKES → ABOUT 3 DOZEN COOKIES**

INGREDIENTS

COOKIES

2 cups all-purpose flour
½ teaspoon baking soda
¼ teaspoon salt
¾ cup (1½ sticks) butter, softened
1 cup granulated sugar
2 large eggs
½ cup low-fat buttermilk

ICING

1 package (16 ounces) confectioners' sugar
2 tablespoons light corn syrup
2 tablespoons milk
⅛ teaspoon salt
assorted food colorings

EACH COOKIE

Calories: About 140
Protein: 1G
Carbohydrates: 25G
Total Fat: 4G
(Saturated Fat: 3G)
Fiber: 0G
Sodium: 75MG

1. **Prepare Cookies:** Arrange oven racks in top and bottom thirds of your oven. Preheat oven to 350°F. Line 2 large cookie sheets with parchment paper.

2. In medium bowl with wire whisk, mix flour, baking soda, and salt. In large bowl with mixer on medium speed, beat butter and granulated sugar for 3 minutes or until fluffy. Add eggs, 1 at a time. Reduce speed to low. Alternately add flour mixture and buttermilk, beginning and ending with flour mixture, just until blended. Drop dough by rounded tablespoonfuls on prepared cookie sheets, 2 inches apart.

3. Bake for 13 to 15 minutes or until golden, rotating cookie sheets between upper and lower racks halfway through baking. Transfer cookies to wire racks and cool completely.

4. **Prepare Icing:** In large bowl with mixer on low speed, beat confectioners' sugar, corn syrup, milk, and salt until smooth. Tint half the icing in bowls with food coloring, as desired. Spread icing on cookies' flat sides. Let stand for 30 minutes or until set.

Double Chocolate Chip
COOKIES

Chocolate chip cookies don't get old, and they probably never will! Here's a tasty take on America's most popular cookie, combining semisweet and white chocolate chips for a delicious double-chocolate sensation.

ACTIVE TIME → 20 MINUTES   TOTAL TIME → 40 MINUTES (PLUS COOLING)   MAKES → ABOUT 2 DOZEN COOKIES

INGREDIENTS

1½ cups all-purpose flour

¾ cup packed brown sugar

½ cup (1 stick)
  butter, softened (no
  substitutions)

¼ cup granulated sugar

2½ teaspoons vanilla
  extract

½ teaspoon baking soda

¼ teaspoon salt

1 large egg

¾ cup semisweet
  chocolate chips

¾ cup white chocolate
  chips

EACH COOKIE

Calories: About 160

Protein: 2G

Carbohydrates: 21G

Total Fat: 8G

(Saturated Fat: 3G)

Fiber: 1G

Sodium: 105MG

1. Preheat oven to 375°F.

2. In large bowl with mixer on medium speed, beat all ingredients except semisweet and white chocolate chips until blended and smooth, occasionally scraping bowl with rubber spatula. With spoon, stir in chips.

3. Drop dough by rounded tablespoonfuls onto large ungreased cookie sheet, 2 inches apart. Bake for 10 to 12 minutes or until golden. With metal spatula, immediately transfer cookies to wire rack to cool. Repeat with remaining dough. Cookies can be made ahead and stored in an airtight container at room temperature for up to 1 week.

SMART CHEF! This recipe works with any combo of chips. Try bittersweet chocolate and butterscotch, or peanut butter and milk chocolate chips. Experiment with different combinations until you find your favorite.

Lemon-Walnut
BISCOTTI

These twice-baked, lemony cookies will stay fresh in the cookie jar for weeks!
But if some hungry cookie-lovers get to them first, they might not last as long. . . .

ACTIVE TIME → 30 MINUTES   TOTAL TIME → 1 HOUR 20 MINUTES (PLUS COOLING)   MAKES → 4 DOZEN BISCOTTI

INGREDIENTS

2 lemons
3¼ cups all-purpose flour
1 tablespoon baking
  powder
½ teaspoon salt
1¼ cups sugar
¾ cup (1½ sticks) butter,
  melted
3 large eggs
1½ cups walnuts (6
  ounces), toasted and
  coarsely chopped

EACH BISCOTTI

Calories: About 120
Protein: 2G
Carbohydrates: 14G
Total Fat: 7G
(Saturated Fat: 3G)
Fiber: 1G
Sodium: 90MG

1. Arrange oven racks in top and bottom thirds of oven. Preheat oven to 350°F. From lemons, grate 1 tablespoon plus 1 teaspoon peel and squeeze 2 tablespoons juice.

2. In medium bowl with wire whisk, mix flour, baking powder, and salt. In large bowl with whisk, mix sugar, melted butter, eggs, and lemon peel and juice until smooth. With spoon, stir flour mixture and walnuts into egg mixture until dough forms.

3. Divide dough in half. On 2 large ungreased cookie sheets, with floured hands, shape each piece of dough into a 4 x 4-inch log on cookie sheet.

4. Bake for 25 to 30 minutes or until golden and toothpick inserted in center of logs comes out clean, rotating cookie sheets between upper and lower racks halfway through baking. Cool logs on cookie sheets on wire racks for 20 minutes. Reduce oven temperature to 325°F.

5. Transfer logs to cutting board. With serrated knife, cut each log crosswise into ½-inch-thick diagonal slices. Place slices, cut side down, on same cookie sheets.

6. Bake slices for 25 to 30 minutes longer or until golden on bottom, rotating cookie sheets between upper and lower racks halfway through baking. With a metal spatula, transfer biscotti to wire racks to cool completely. Biscotti can be placed in airtight container and stored at room temperature for up to 2 weeks, or in freezer for up to 6 months.

Blueberry-Spice
WHOOPIE PIES

A whoopie pie is like a sandwich, but for dessert! It's made with two soft cookies and
a fluffy white icing. This summery version is packed with fresh blueberries.

ACTIVE TIME → 30 MINUTES   **TOTAL TIME** → 1 HOUR 5 MINUTES (PLUS COOLING)   **MAKES** → 15 WHOOPIE PIES

INGREDIENTS
CAKES
nonstick cooking spray
2 cups all-purpose flour
1 teaspoon ground
   cinnamon
½ teaspoon ground ginger
½ teaspoon baking soda
¼ teaspoon ground
   nutmeg
¼ teaspoon salt
⅛ teaspoon ground cloves
¾ cup (1½ sticks) butter,
   softened
1 cup packed light
   brown sugar
1 large egg
2 tablespoons light
   (mild) molasses
½ cup reduced-fat
   sour cream

1. **Prepare Cakes:** Preheat oven to 350°F. Spray 3 large cookie sheets
with nonstick cooking spray. In medium bowl with wire whisk, mix flour,
cinnamon, ginger, baking soda, nutmeg, salt, and cloves.

2. In large bowl with mixer on medium-high speed, beat butter until smooth.
Add sugar and beat for 3 to 4 minutes or until light and fluffy, occasionally
scraping bowl with rubber spatula. Add egg and molasses; beat until well
blended. Reduce speed to low; alternately add flour mixture and sour cream,
beginning and ending with flour mixture, just until blended, occasionally
scraping bowl.

3. Spoon batter by heaping tablespoonfuls onto prepared cookie sheets,
2½ inches apart (you should get 30 cakes). Bake cakes, one sheet at a
time, for 11 to 13 minutes or until cakes spring back when pressed lightly.
Cool for 1 minute, on cookie sheet, on wire rack; with metal spatula,
transfer cakes to wire racks to cool completely. Cakes can be made ahead,
wrapped tightly in plastic wrap, and stored at room temperature up to
1 day.

FILLING

1 package (8 ounces)
   reduced-fat cream cheese
1 jar (7 ounces)
   marshmallow cream
   (about 1½ cups)
2 cups fresh blueberries,
   plus additional for
   garnish

EACH WHOOPIE PIE

Calories: About 320
Protein: 4G
Carbohydrates: 44G
Total Fat: 15G
(Saturated Fat: 9G)
Fiber: 1G
Sodium: 260MG

4. Prepare Filling: In large bowl with mixer on medium-high speed, beat cream cheese until smooth. Reduce speed to low; add marshmallow cream; beat just until blended, scraping beaters if necessary. Fold in blueberries. Spread ¼ cup filling on flat side of half the cakes. Top each with plain cake, flat side down, pressing lightly. Garnish with additional blueberries pressed into side of filling.

31

Swap-It-Your-Way
SWEET & SALTY COOKIES

Let nothing go to waste! Take your pick of veggie scraps (like zucchini or carrots), scour your pantry for something that can be made into a chunky texture (like pretzels and peanuts), then follow this recipe. Our Ingredient Swap Guide offers more flavorful combos to try.

ACTIVE TIME → 15 MINUTES   TOTAL TIME → 35 MINUTES (PLUS COOLING)   MAKES → 2 DOZEN COOKIES

INGREDIENTS

3⅓ cups all-purpose flour

⅓ cup cornstarch

1½ teaspoons baking powder

1¼ teaspoons baking soda

1½ teaspoons salt

1¼ cup (2½ sticks) butter, softened

1½ cups packed brown sugar

¾ cup granulated sugar

2 large eggs

1 tablespoon vanilla extract

1 cup Veggie Scraps (such as grated zucchini)

1½ cups Chunks (¾ cup chopped peanuts plus ¾ cup broken pretzels)

EACH COOKIE

Calories: About 275
Protein: 4G
Carbohydrates: 38G
Total Fat: 13G
(Saturated Fat: 7G)
Fiber: 1G
Sodium: 265MG

1. Arrange oven racks in the top and bottom thirds of the oven. Preheat oven to 350°F. In a medium bowl with a wire whisk, mix flour, cornstarch, baking powder, baking soda, and salt.

2. In a large bowl with mixer on medium speed, beat butter and sugars until light and fluffy. Beat in the eggs, 1 at a time. Beat in vanilla, then flour mixture just until blended. Fold in Veggie Scraps and Chunks.

3. Scoop dough by *scant* (or just barely full) ⅓ cup cupfuls onto 2 large ungreased cookie sheets, about 1 inch apart. Bake for 20 to 25 minutes, or until bottoms are golden brown, rotating cookie sheets between upper and lower racks halfway through baking. Cool cookies completely, on cookie sheets, on wire racks.

→ Loaded Chocolate Chip Cookies

Prepare cookies as directed, but use 1 cup carrot peels for Veggie Scraps and 1 cup chocolate chips and ½ cup chopped walnuts for Chunks.

Ingredient Swap Guide

1 CUP VEGGIES

- grated zucchini
- chopped carrot peels
- grated summer squash
- corn kernels

1½ CUPS CHUNKS

- chopped nuts
- broken pretzels
- chocolate chips
- toffee bits
- granola
- potato chips

Classic
BROWNIES

Go wild and serve these brownies topped with vanilla ice cream and our Chocolate Shell. Drizzle this ooey-gooey goodness on any treat—and watch it harden like magic! Also try the Praline-Iced Brownies for a fun twist. Serve fresh to get the full hot brownie, cold ice cream effect.

ACTIVE TIME → 15 MINUTES   TOTAL TIME → 40 MINUTES (PLUS COOLING)   MAKES → 24 BROWNIES

INGREDIENTS

¾ cup (1½ sticks) butter

4 ounces unsweetened chocolate

4 ounces semisweet chocolate

2 cups sugar

1 tablespoon vanilla extract

5 large eggs

1¼ cups all-purpose flour

½ teaspoon salt

vanilla ice cream, optional

GH Chocolate Shell, opposite, and ice cream, optional

EACH BROWNIE WITHOUT TOPPINGS

Calories: About 205
Protein: 3G
Carbohydrates: 25G
Total Fat: 11G
(Saturated Fat: 7G)
Fiber: 1G
Sodium: 125MG

1. Preheat oven to 350°F. Grease a 13 x 9-inch metal baking pan.

2. In 3-quart saucepan, melt butter and chocolates over medium-low heat, stirring frequently. Remove saucepan from heat; stir in sugar and vanilla. Stir in eggs, 1 at a time, until well blended. Stir in flour and salt just until blended. Spread batter in prepared baking pan.

3. Bake for 25 to 30 minutes or until toothpick inserted in brownies 2 inches from edge comes out almost clean. Cool brownies completely in pan on wire rack.

4. When cool, cut brownies lengthwise into 4 strips, then cut each strip crosswise into 6 pieces. Top each brownie with ice cream and GH Chocolate Shell, if using.

→ Chocolate Shell

In medium microwave-safe bowl, combine **8 ounces good-quality semisweet (50–65 percent cacao) chocolate**, coarsely chopped, and **¾ cup refined coconut oil**. Microwave on high in 20-second intervals or until melted, stirring in between. Cool completely before using. If necessary, reheat 10 to 20 seconds to remelt to pouring consistency. Mixture can be made ahead, placed in airtight container, and stored at room temperature up to 2 weeks. Makes 1¾ cups of mixture, or about 8 shells.

→ Praline-Iced Brownies

Prepare Classic Brownies as directed. When brownies are cool, in 2-quart saucepan, heat **5 tablespoons butter** and **⅓ cup packed brown sugar** over medium-low heat for 5 minutes or until sugar melts and mixture boils, stirring occasionally. Remove pan from heat. Whisk in **1 tablespoon vanilla extract**, **2 tablespoons water**, and **2 cups confectioners' sugar** until smooth. Spread icing over brownies; sprinkle with **½ cup pecans**, toasted and chopped, pressing lightly with your hands so they adhere. Cut brownies lengthwise into 8 strips, then cut each strip crosswise into 8 pieces. Makes 24 brownies.

EACH BROWNIE: About 300 Calories, 3G Protein, 39G Carbohydrate, 15G Total Fat (8G Saturated), 2G Fiber, 130MG Sodium

Rocky Road
BROWNIES

You'll find all the lusciousness of rocky road ice cream in these fudge-tastic treats.

ACTIVE TIME → 25 MINUTES   TOTAL TIME → 50 MINUTES (PLUS COOLING)   MAKES → 24 BROWNIES

INGREDIENTS

1¼ cups all-purpose flour

½ teaspoon baking powder

½ teaspoon salt

¾ cup (1½ sticks) butter

6 ounces unsweetened chocolate

2 cups sugar

2 teaspoons vanilla extract

5 large eggs

2 cups miniature marshmallows

1½ cups assorted nuts, toasted and coarsely chopped

EACH BROWNIE

Calories: About 255
Protein: 5G
Carbohydrates: 29G
Total Fat: 15G
(Saturated Fat: 7G)
Fiber: 2G
Sodium: 150MG

1. Preheat oven to 350°F. Grease a 13 x 9-inch metal baking pan.

2. In medium bowl with wire whisk, mix flour, baking powder, and salt. In 3-quart saucepan, melt butter and chocolate over medium-low heat, stirring frequently. Remove saucepan from heat; stir in sugar and vanilla. Stir in eggs, 1 at a time, until well blended. Stir in flour mixture just until blended. Spread batter in prepared baking pan.

3. Bake for 20 minutes or until toothpick inserted in brownies 2 inches from edge comes out almost clean. Sprinkle brownies evenly with marshmallows; top with nuts. Bake for 5 minutes longer or until marshmallows melt slightly. Cool brownies completely in pan on wire rack.

4. When cool, cut brownies lengthwise into 4 strips, then cut each strip crosswise into 6 pieces.

German Chocolate
BROWNIES

Making a German chocolate cake is super-complicated—but not this bite-size brownie version, topped with a gooey layer of coconut and pecans. Skip the difficulty, but keep the delicious!

ACTIVE TIME → **25 MINUTES**   **TOTAL TIME** → **1 HOUR 10 MINUTES** (PLUS COOLING)   **MAKES** → **36 BROWNIES**

INGREDIENTS
BROWNIES

½ cup (1 stick) butter

8 ounces (2 packages) sweet baking chocolate

1 cup packed brown sugar

3 large eggs

1 teaspoon vanilla extract

1 cup all-purpose flour

½ teaspoon salt

GERMAN CHOCOLATE TOPPING

3 large egg whites

2 cups sweetened flaked coconut

1 cup pecans, toasted and chopped

½ cup packed brown sugar

¼ cup whole milk

½ teaspoon vanilla extract

⅛ teaspoon almond extract

⅛ teaspoon salt

EACH BROWNIE

Calories: About 150
Protein: 2G
Carbohydrates: 18G
Total Fat: 8G (Saturated Fat: 4G)
Fiber: 1G
Sodium: 85MG

1. Preheat oven to 350°F. Grease a 13 x 9-inch metal baking pan.

2. Prepare Brownies: In 3-quart saucepan, melt butter and chocolate over medium-low heat, stirring frequently. Remove saucepan from heat; stir in sugar. Stir in eggs, 1 at a time, until well blended. Add vanilla. Stir in flour and salt just until blended. Spread batter in prepared baking pan.

3. Prepare German Chocolate Topping: In medium bowl with wire whisk, beat egg whites until foamy. Stir in coconut, pecans, sugar, milk, extracts, and salt until well combined. Spread topping evenly over brownies.

4. Bake for 45 to 50 minutes or until toothpick inserted in brownies 2 inches from edge comes out almost clean and topping turns golden brown. Cool brownies completely in pan on wire rack.

HOW TO: SOFTEN BROWN SUGAR

Ready to bake but your brown sugar is hard as a rock? Place the hard chunk in a microwave-safe bowl and cover with a damp (not wet) paper towel. Microwave on high 30 seconds and repeat just until soft; use immediately.

Super Simple
BROWNIES!

Baking from scratch is fun, but it can be very time-consuming, not to mention complicated. If you're strapped for time, or if you just want something easy, here are some recipes that start with a mix.

Hazelnut Brownies

Prepare **1 box (19.5 to 22.5 ounces) family-size brownie mix** as label directs. Stir in **1 cup hazelnuts**, toasted and coarsely chopped, and ½ **cup chocolate-hazelnut spread** (about half a 13-ounce jar) until blended. Spread batter in greased 13 x 9-inch metal baking pan. Bake for 25 to 30 minutes or until toothpick inserted 2 inches from edge of brownies comes out almost clean. Cool in pan. Makes 24. See opposite page for recipe photo.

EACH BROWNIE: About 225 Calories, 3G Protein, 26G Carbohydrate, 13G Total Fat (2G Saturated), 2G Fiber, 107MG Sodium

Swirl Brownies

Prepare **1 box (19.8 ounces) brownie mix** as label directs for 9 x 9-inch metal baking pan. In medium bowl, mix ½ **cup peanut butter**, ¼ **cup confectioners' sugar**, **1½ tablespoons melted butter**, and **1 large egg** until smooth. Dollop peanut butter mixture onto brownie batter in pan; swirl with knife. Bake according to package directions. Makes 16.

EACH BROWNIE: About 280 Calories, 4G Protein, 33G Carbohydrate, 15G Total Fat (3G Saturated), 0G Fiber, 170MG Sodium

Black-Bottom Brownies

Preheat oven to 350°F. Prepare **1 box (18 ounces) brownie mix** as label directs for 9 x 9-inch metal baking pan. Beat **1 package (8 ounces) cream cheese**, **1 large egg**, and ½ **cup sugar** with mixer until smooth; pour over brownie batter in pan. Bake for 45 minutes or until toothpick inserted in brownies 2 inches from edge comes out almost clean. Makes 16.

EACH BROWNIE: About 275 Calories, 3G Protein, 35G Carbohydrate, 14G Total Fat (4G Saturated), 0G Fiber, 170MG Sodium

Raspberry-Rhubarb
CRUMB BARS

Haven't tried rhubarb yet? Once you taste these buttery bars with ruby-red filling, you'll be a fan forever.

ACTIVE TIME → 30 MINUTES   **TOTAL TIME** → 1 HOUR 25 MINUTES (PLUS COOLING)   **MAKES** → 16 BARS

INGREDIENTS

1¾ cups all-purpose flour

¾ cup packed light brown sugar

½ teaspoon baking soda

½ teaspoon salt

¾ cup (1½ sticks) cold butter, cut up

½ cup sliced almonds

2 cups sliced rhubarb stems, sliced ½ inch thick (about 10 ounces)

2 cups raspberries

¾ cup granulated sugar

2 tablespoons cornstarch

2 tablespoons fresh orange juice

2 teaspoons vanilla extract

EACH BAR

Calories: About 235
Protein: 3G
Carbohydrates: 34G
Total Fat: 10G
(Saturated Fat: 6G)
Fiber: 2G
Sodium: 190MG

1. Preheat oven to 350°F. Line 8 x 8-inch metal baking pan with parchment paper, extending 2 inches over rim.

2. In food processor with knife blade attached, pulse flour, brown sugar, baking soda, and salt until combined. Add butter and pulse just until dough resembles coarse crumbs. Press ⅔ of dough into bottom of prepared baking pan. Bake 15 minutes or until pale golden; place on a wire rack to cool until warm but not hot.

3. Stir almonds into remaining crumb mixture; press to form large crumbs.

4. In large bowl, combine rhubarb, raspberries, granulated sugar, cornstarch, orange juice, and vanilla; spread over warm crust. Sprinkle with crumb topping.

5. Bake 40 to 45 minutes or until filling is bubbling. Cool bars completely, in pan, on wire rack. When cool, using parchment, transfer bars to cutting board. Cut into 16 squares.

?

WHAT IS IT?

RHUBARB is a plant with bright red stalks that looks like celery, but the leaves are inedible. A spring/summer veggie with a tart flavor, it's often paired with fruit, like strawberries and raspberries, in dessert recipes.

FUN FOOD!

PB&J BARS

This twist on the classic peanut-butter-and-jelly will have friends and family raving about your baking skills. Think of it as a sandwich but for dessert.

ACTIVE TIME → **30 MINUTES**   **TOTAL TIME** → **1 HOUR 15 MINUTES** (PLUS COOLING)   **MAKES** → **24 BARS**

INGREDIENTS

1 cup butter
  (2 sticks), softened
  (no substitutions)
1 cup sugar
½ cup creamy peanut
  butter
1 large egg
3 cups all-purpose flour
1 cup salted, dry-roasted
  peanuts, coarsely
  chopped
1 cup grape or strawberry
  jam

EACH BAR

Calories: About 260
Protein: 5G
Carbohydrates: 31G
Total Fat: 14G
(Saturated Fat: 6G)
Fiber: 1G
Sodium: 165MG

1. Preheat oven to 350°F. Line 13 x 9-inch metal baking pan with foil; grease foil.

2. In large bowl with mixer on low speed, beat butter and sugar until mixed, occasionally scraping bowl with rubber spatula. Increase speed to high; beat until light and fluffy. Reduce speed to low; beat in peanut butter, then egg until well combined, occasionally scraping bowl. Beat in flour just until evenly moistened (dough will be crumbly). Beat in peanuts.

3. Reserve 2 cups dough. Press remaining dough into prepared baking pan into even layer. Spread jam over dough in pan. With your hands, break the reserved 2 cups of dough into large chunks (about ¾-inch pieces). Drop chunks over jam, leaving spaces between clumps of dough; do not pat down.

4. Bake for 45 to 50 minutes or until golden. Cool bars completely, in pan, on wire rack.

5. When cool, using foil, transfer bars to cutting board. Cut bars lengthwise into 3 strips, then cut each strip crosswise into 8 pieces.

Butterscotch
BLONDIES

Brown sugar keeps these bars super-moist. For even more of that rich butterscotch flavor, opt for dark brown sugar.

ACTIVE TIME → 15 MINUTES   TOTAL TIME → 35 MINUTES (PLUS COOLING)   MAKES → 24 BLONDIES

INGREDIENTS

1 cup all-purpose flour
2 teaspoons baking powder
¾ teaspoon salt
6 tablespoons butter
1¾ cups packed light brown sugar
2 teaspoons vanilla extract
2 large eggs, lightly beaten
1 cup pecans, coarsely chopped

EACH BAR

Calories: About 145
Protein: 2G
Carbohydrates: 20G
Total Fat: 7G
(Saturated Fat: 2G)
Fiber: 1G
Sodium: 150MG

1. Preheat oven to 350°F. Grease 13 x 9-inch metal baking pan.

2. In medium bowl with wire whisk, mix flour, baking powder, and salt. In 3-quart saucepan, melt butter over medium heat. Remove saucepan from heat; stir in sugar and vanilla. Add eggs; stir until well mixed. Stir in flour mixture and pecans just until blended. Spread batter in prepared baking pan.

3. Bake for 20 to 25 minutes or until toothpick inserted in blondies 2 inches from edge comes out almost clean. Do not overbake; blondies will become firm as they cool. Cool blondies completely, in pan, on wire rack.

4. When cool, cut blondies lengthwise into 4 strips, then cut each strip crosswise into 6 pieces.

SMART CHEF! Like chocolate in your blondies? Prepare the recipe as directed, but sprinkle the batter with ⅓ cup mini chocolate chips before baking.

Granola
BARS

Bake a pan of these treats and you'll never go back to the packaged stuff.
These are great for breakfast or as a midday snack.

ACTIVE TIME → 15 MINUTES   **TOTAL TIME →** 50 MINUTES (PLUS COOLING)   **MAKES →** 18 BARS

INGREDIENTS

nonstick cooking spray
2 cups old-fashioned oats, uncooked
¾ cup toasted wheat germ
¾ cup chopped walnuts
¾ cup dried cranberries
2 tablespoons packed light brown sugar
1 teaspoon ground cinnamon
½ teaspoon salt
½ cup honey
½ cup vegetable oil
2 large egg whites

EACH BAR

Calories: About 190
Protein: 4G
Carbohydrates: 23G
Total Fat: 10G
(Saturated Fat: 1G)
Fiber: 2G
Sodium: 70MG

1. Preheat oven to 325°F. Line a 13 x 9-inch metal baking pan with foil, extending 2 inches over rim; spray foil with nonstick cooking spray.

2. In glass pie plate, spread oats. Microwave on high in 1-minute intervals for 4 to 5 minutes or until fragrant and golden, stirring occasionally. Cool to room temperature.

3. In large bowl, mix oats, wheat germ, walnuts, cranberries, brown sugar, cinnamon, and salt. Stir in honey, oil, and egg whites until well mixed. Transfer to prepared pan. Using wet hands, press into even layer.

4. Bake for 32 to 35 minutes or until dark golden. Cool granola completely, in pan, on wire rack.

5. When cool, lift foil and transfer granola to cutting board. Cut lengthwise into 6 strips, then cut each strip crosswise into thirds. (You should have roughly 4¼ x 1½-inch bars.) Bars can be made ahead, placed in airtight container, and stored at room temperature for up to 1 week or frozen for up to 1 month.

2

Cakes & Pies

Master the art of making a cake or pie from scratch and consider yourself an all-star baker. It's easy to score a home run with simple recipes like our Cinnamon Crumb Cake, whimsical Flowerpot Cupcakes (from a mix!), or Peachy Pecan Crumb Pie. If you're feeling more ambitious, try our New York–Style Cheesecake or Mixed-Berry Pie. Not in the mood for sweets? No worries! Savory quiches start with a store-bought crust for maximum simplicity, and are filled with ingredients like ham and spinach or pimento cheese for maximum flavor.

Cinnamon
CRUMB CAKE

This extra-tender sour cream cake is crowned with a crunchy cinnamon-pecan topping.
Serve it for breakfast or as an afterschool treat.

ACTIVE TIME → 25 MINUTES   TOTAL TIME → 1 HOUR 5 MINUTES (PLUS COOLING)   MAKES → 10 SERVINGS

INGREDIENTS

CRUMB TOPPING

½ cup pecans, toasted and
  chopped
⅓ cup packed dark brown
  sugar
¼ cup all-purpose flour
½ teaspoon ground
  cinnamon
2 tablespoons butter

CAKE

1½ cups all-purpose flour
1 teaspoon baking powder
¼ teaspoon baking soda
¼ teaspoon salt
¾ cup granulated sugar
4 tablespoons butter
1 teaspoon vanilla extract
2 large eggs
⅔ cup sour cream

1. Prepare Crumb Topping: In small bowl, mix pecans, brown sugar, flour, and cinnamon until well blended. With your fingertips, work in softened butter until mixture resembles marbles.

2. Prepare Cake: Preheat oven to 350°F. Grease 9-inch springform pan and dust with flour. In medium bowl with wire whisk, mix flour, baking powder, baking soda, and salt.

3. In large bowl with mixer on medium speed, beat granulated sugar, butter, and vanilla for 5 to 6 minutes or until mixture is light and fluffy, occasionally scraping bowl with rubber spatula. Reduce mixer speed to low; add eggs, 1 at a time, beating well after each addition.

4. With mixer on low speed, alternately add flour mixture and sour cream, beginning and ending with flour mixture, just until smooth, occasionally scraping down side of bowl with rubber spatula.

5. Pour batter into prepared springform pan. Sprinkle evenly with crumb topping and gently press into batter. Bake for 40 to 45 minutes or until toothpick inserted in center of cake comes out clean. Cool cake, in pan,

EACH SERVING

Calories: About 300
Protein: 5G
Carbohydrates: 37G
Total Fat: 15G
(Saturated Fat: 7G)
Fiber: 1G
Sodium: 225MG

on wire rack. With small metal spatula, loosen cake from side of pan and remove springform ring. Cake can be made ahead, wrapped tightly in plastic wrap, and frozen for up to 1 month.

WHAT IS IT?

A **SPRINGFORM PAN** is a round, deep cake pan with a removable bottom and a collar that snaps open. The springform ring is held together with an adjustable latch or buckle. Springform pans are ideal for crumb-topped cakes, cheesecakes, or any time you need to remove a cake from its pan without having to turn it upside down.

Chocolate
LAYER CAKE

In this recipe, the batter is blended with buttermilk for maximum moistness.
The cocoa in the frosting gives the cake an intense chocolate flavor.

ACTIVE TIME → 45 MINUTES   **TOTAL TIME → 1 HOUR 15 MINUTES** (PLUS COOLING)   **MAKES → 16 SERVINGS**

INGREDIENTS
CAKE LAYERS

2 cups all-purpose flour

1 cup unsweetened cocoa

1½ teaspoons baking
soda

¼ teaspoon salt

¾ cup (1½ sticks) butter,
softened, plus more for
greasing the pan

1 cup packed brown
sugar

1 cup granulated sugar

3 large eggs

2 teaspoons vanilla
extract

1½ cups low-fat
buttermilk

FROSTING

⅓ cup unsweetened
cocoa

1 cup (2 sticks) butter,
softened

2 tablespoons
confectioners' sugar

12 ounces semisweet
chocolate, melted and
cooled

1. Prepare Cake Layers: Preheat oven to 350°F. Grease three 8-inch-round cake pans. Line bottoms with waxed paper; grease paper. Dust pans with flour.

2. In large bowl with wire whisk, mix flour, cocoa, baking soda, and salt. In another large bowl with mixer on low speed, beat butter and sugars until blended. Increase speed to high; beat for 5 minutes or until mixture is pale and fluffy, occasionally scraping down sides of bowl with rubber spatula. Reduce mixer speed to medium-low; add eggs, 1 at a time, beating well after each addition. Beat in vanilla. Alternately, add flour mixture and buttermilk, beginning and ending with flour mixture, just until smooth, occasionally scraping down sides of bowl with rubber spatula.

3. Spoon batter evenly among prepared cake pans. Bake for 22 to 25 minutes or until toothpick inserted in center of cakes comes out clean. Cool cakes, in pans, on wire racks for 10 minutes. With small knife, loosen cake layers from sides of pans, and turn cake layers over onto wire racks. Carefully remove and discard waxed paper; cool completely, about 45 minutes. Cakes can be made ahead, wrapped tightly in plastic wrap, and stored at room temperature for up to 1 day or frozen for up to 1 month. Bring to room temperature before frosting cake.

EACH SERVING

Calories: About 495
Protein: 7G
Carbohydrates: 55G
Total Fat: 30G
(Saturated Fat: 18G)
Fiber: 4G
Sodium: 415MG

4. **Prepare Frosting:** Meanwhile, in small bowl, mix cocoa and ⅓ cup boiling water, stirring until smooth. In large bowl, with mixer on medium-high speed, beat butter and confectioners' sugar for 5 minutes or until fluffy. Reduce speed to medium-low; add melted chocolate, then cocoa mixture, beating until smooth and occasionally scraping down sides of bowl with rubber spatula. If frosting is too runny, refrigerate until just stiff enough to spread.

5. **Assemble Cake:** Place 1 cake layer, bottom side up, on cake plate; spread with ⅓ cup frosting. Top with second layer, bottom side up; spread with ⅓ cup frosting. Place remaining layer, bottom side up, on top. Spread remaining frosting over sides and top of cake.

SMART CHEF! For evenly baked cakes, stagger the cake pans on two oven racks during baking. Place two on the upper rack, leaving space in the center, and one on the lower rack in the center. This way, the top pans are not directly above the bottom one.

Carrot CAKE

Instead of a typical layer cake with frosting, our carrot cake is prepared in a Bundt pan, then topped with a simple cream cheese glaze.

ACTIVE TIME → 20 MINUTES   **TOTAL TIME** → 1 HOUR 5 MINUTES (PLUS COOLING)   **MAKES** → 16 SERVINGS

INGREDIENTS
CAKE

2¼ cups all-purpose flour
2 teaspoons baking soda
2 teaspoons ground cinnamon
1 teaspoon ground ginger
1 teaspoon baking powder
1 teaspoon salt
2 large eggs
2 large egg whites
1 cup granulated sugar
¾ cup packed dark brown sugar
1 (8- to 8¼-ounce) can crushed pineapple in juice
⅓ cup canola oil
1 tablespoon vanilla extract
1 bag (10 ounces) shredded carrots
½ cup dark raisins

CREAM CHEESE ICING

2 ounces cream cheese
¾ cup confectioners' sugar
½ tsp milk
¼ teaspoon vanilla extract

1. Prepare Cake: Preheat oven to 350°F. Grease and flour 12-cup Bundt pan.

2. In medium bowl with wire whisk, mix flour, baking soda, cinnamon, ginger, baking powder, and salt.

3. In large bowl with mixer on medium speed, beat eggs and egg whites until blended. Beat in sugars; beat for 2 minutes. Reduce speed to low; beat in pineapple with juice, oil, and vanilla. Add flour mixture; beat for 1 minute. Stir in carrots and raisins.

4. Pour batter into prepared Bundt pan. Bake 45 to 50 minutes or until toothpick inserted in center comes out clean. Cool in pan on wire rack for 10 minutes. With small knife, loosen cake from sides of pan; turn upside down onto wire rack, removing from pan, and let cool completely.

5. Prepare Cream Cheese Icing: In bowl, stir cream cheese and ¼ cup confectioners' sugar until smooth. Add milk, vanilla, and remaining ½ cup confectioners' sugar; stir to a drizzling consistency. Drizzle icing over cake.

EACH SERVING

Calories: About 275
Protein: 4G
Carbohydrates: 51G
Total Fat: 7G
(Saturated Fat: 1G)
Fiber: 1G
Sodium: 381MG

Cranberry Cake
WITH ALMOND GLAZE

In the fall, when fresh cranberries are in season, buy an extra bag or two to stash
in the freezer so you can bake this cake any time.

ACTIVE TIME → 35 MINUTES   TOTAL TIME → 1 HOUR (PLUS COOLING)   MAKES → 16 SERVINGS

INGREDIENTS

1 lemon

2 cups fresh or frozen
cranberries

2¼ cups granulated sugar

⅛ teaspoon ground
cinnamon

3 cups all-purpose flour,
plus more for dusting

1 teaspoon baking powder

½ teaspoon baking soda

½ teaspoon salt

1 cup (2 sticks) butter (no
substitutions), softened,
plus more for greasing
the pan

1 package (8 ounces)
cream cheese, softened

6 large eggs, at room
temperature

1 tablespoon plus ¼
teaspoon vanilla extract

1¼ teaspoons almond
extract

1 cup confectioners' sugar

sliced almonds, for
garnish, optional

1. Preheat oven to 350°F. From lemon, grate ¼ teaspoon peel and squeeze 2
teaspoons juice. Set lemon juice aside.

2. In 2-quart saucepan, combine 1 cup cranberries, ¼ cup granulated sugar,
lemon peel, and cinnamon. Cook over medium-low heat for 10 minutes or
until some cranberries burst, stirring frequently. Cool completely. Stir in
remaining 1 cup cranberries. Cranberry mixture can be made ahead, placed
in an airtight container, and refrigerated for up to 3 days.

3. Meanwhile, grease 12-cup Bundt pan and then dust lightly with flour. In
large bowl with wire whisk, mix flour, baking powder, baking soda, and salt.

4. In another large bowl with mixer on medium-high speed, beat butter
and cream cheese until fluffy and smooth. With mixer running, add 2 cups
granulated sugar, ½ cup at a time. Beat for 1 minute. Add eggs, 1 at a time,
occasionally scraping down sides of bowl with rubber spatula. Beat in 1
tablespoon vanilla and 1 teaspoon almond extract. Reduce mixer speed to
low; gradually beat in flour mixture just until combined.

5. Spoon ¾ of batter into prepared Bundt pan. Spread cooled cranberry
mixture over batter in even layer. Top with remaining batter. Bake for 55
minutes to 1 hour 10 minutes or until toothpick inserted in center of cake
comes out clean. Cool cake, in pan, on wire rack for 10 minutes. With small

knife, loosen cake from sides of pan, and turn over onto wire rack. Remove pan and cool cake completely. Cake may be made ahead, wrapped tightly in plastic wrap, and stored at room temperature for up to 1 day.

6. To serve, in medium bowl with wire whisk, mix confectioners' sugar, reserved 2 teaspoons lemon juice, 1 tablespoon water, and remaining ¼ teaspoon vanilla extract and ¼ teaspoon almond extract until smooth; drizzle over cake. Garnish with almonds, if using.

?

WHAT IS IT?

A **BUNDT PAN** is a cast-aluminum, tube-shaped baking pan with a fluted or ridged design on the bottom and sides. This is what gives a Bundt cake its distinct, impressive look.

Epic
POUND CAKE

One batter, three ways! Try this outstanding original recipe, or choose from
a trio of fruity variations.

ACTIVE TIME → 15 MINUTES   TOTAL TIME → 1 HOUR 20 MINUTES (PLUS COOLING)   MAKES → 10 SERVINGS

INGREDIENTS

1½ cups all-purpose flour
¼ teaspoon baking soda
¼ teaspoon salt
1 cup granulated sugar
½ cup (1 stick) butter,
   softened
4 ounces cream cheese,
   softened
1 teaspoon freshly grated
   lemon peel
3 large eggs, at room
   temperature
2 teaspoons vanilla extract

EACH SERVING

Calories: About 290
Protein: 3G
Carbohydrates: 35G
Total Fat: 15G
(Saturated Fat: 9G)
Fiber: 2G
Sodium: 215MG

1. Preheat oven to 325°F. Grease 8½ x 4½-inch loaf pan, and dust lightly with flour.

2. In large bowl with wire whisk, mix flour, baking soda, and salt. In another large bowl, with mixer on medium speed, beat sugar, butter, cream cheese, and lemon peel until smooth. Beat in eggs, 1 at a time, occasionally scraping down sides of bowl with rubber spatula. Beat in vanilla. In 2 batches, beat in flour mixture until just combined.

3. Scoop batter into prepared loaf pan; smooth top. Bake for 1 hour 5 minutes to 1 hour 10 minutes or until toothpick inserted in center of cake comes out clean. Cool cake, in pan, for 10 minutes on wire rack. Remove cake from pan and cool completely on wire rack.

Raspberry-Lemon Pound Cake

Prepare Epic Pound Cake as directed, but gently fold **1 container (6 ounces) raspberries** into batter before pouring into prepared pan and baking as directed. In blender, puree **½ cup confectioners' sugar**, **5 tablespoons heavy cream**, and **1 tablespoon seedless raspberry jam** until smooth, scraping down sides, as needed. Drizzle glaze over cooled cake. Serves 10.

EACH SERVING: About 355 Calories, 5G Protein, 45G Carbohydrate, 18G Total Fat (10G Saturated), 2G Fiber, 220MG Sodium

Rhubarb Tart

Grease and lightly flour 11-inch tart pan with removable bottom. Place pan on rimmed baking sheet. Prepare batter for Epic Pound Cake as directed, but add **½ teaspoon ground cinnamon** to flour mixture. Pour batter into prepared pan. Arrange **8 ounces rhubarb**, trimmed, cut into 4-inch lengths, and halved lengthwise (quartered, if thick), in spokes on top of batter. Bake for 50 to 55 minutes or until toothpick inserted in center of tart comes out clean. Cool tart completely, in pan, on wire rack. Garnish with **edible flowers**, if desired. Dust lightly with **confectioners' sugar** before serving. Serves 10.

EACH SERVING: About 300 Calories, 5G Protein, 38G Carbohydrate, 15G Total Fat (9G Saturated), 1G Fiber, 220MG Sodium

Triple Citrus Bundt

Grease and flour 12-cup Bundt pan. Prepare Epic Pound Cake as directed, but double batter, adding **1 teaspoon baking powder** to flour mixture. Add **1 teaspoon each grated orange peel and lime peel**, in addition to lemon peel. Bake for 1 hour or until toothpick inserted in center of cake comes out clean. Turn cake upside down onto wire rack; remove pan. Mix **3 tablespoons orange juice, 2 tablespoons each lemon juice and lime juice, and 1¼ cups confectioners' sugar**, sifted, until smooth; brush all over cooled cake. Let cake stand until somewhat set. Garnish with strips of **candied citrus peel**, if desired. Serves 16.

EACH SERVING: About 400 Calories, 6G Protein, 54G Carbohydrate, 18G Total Fat (11G Saturated), 1G Fiber, 305MG Sodium

FUN FOOD!

Flowerpot CUPCAKES

Do you have a green thumb? Even if you don't love gardening, you'll definitely love these cupcakes! This recipe calls for cake mix, so you can focus on the decorations. Shape chewy candy into peapods and carrots, plant them in chocolate-cookie-crumb-topped cupcakes, and dig in!

MAKES → 15 CUPCAKES

INGREDIENTS

nonstick cooking spray

15 flowerpot silicone baking cups (available at wilton.com) or other baking cups

1 (15.25-ounce) box devil's food cake mix

½ (14-ounce) package chocolate sandwich cookies

1 (16-ounce) can chocolate frosting

orange and green fruit chews (such as Starburst®, Airheads®, or Laffy Taffy®)

thin green licorice laces (or green fruit chews cut into thin strips)

green mini candy-coated chocolates

EACH SERVING

Calories: About 360
Protein: 3G
Carbohydrates: 52G
Total Fat: 17G
(Saturated Fat: 4G)
Fiber: 0G
Sodium: 341MG

58

1. Spray baking cups with cooking spray and place on large baking sheet.

2. Prepare cake mix for cupcakes as label directs, dividing batter among prepared baking cups. If you're using flowerpot molds, fill each with *scant* (or just barely full) ⅓ cup batter. Bake the cupcakes as label directs, and cool them on wire rack.

3. Scrape the cream filling from the sandwich cookies and discard it. In food processor with knife blade attached, pulse cookies into fine crumbs (you'll need about ¾ cup) to make "dirt."

4. Spread frosting onto cupcakes; top with cookie crumbs, pressing to adhere.

5. Prepare "Carrots":

Squeeze orange fruit chews (we used Starburst®) to shape them into triangles.

Press horizontal lines with a toothpick into the surface of each "carrot"; poke 2 holes in the top.

Cut and insert 2 small pieces of green licorice lace into the holes in the top of the carrot to make a "stem."

6. Prepare "Pea Pods":

With kitchen shears, cut green fruit chews (we used Airheads®) into small football shapes; mold them with your hands to get the shape just right.

Press 4 to 5 mini candy-coated chocolates (we used M&M's®) onto 1 side of each oval.

Fold the other side over to cover the candies slightly. Cut green licorice laces into various lengths and place around the "pods" to make "vines."

7. Place "carrots" and "pea pods" with their "vines" on cupcakes. Sprinkle "carrots" with more cookie crumbs.

Golden Butter
CUPCAKES

Every junior baker wants a great cupcake recipe—and this one's a winner. Who knows? You just might find yourself in a cupcake battle on reality television one day, and it's never too early to start practicing.

ACTIVE TIME → 15 MINUTES   **TOTAL TIME →** 35 MINUTES (PLUS COOLING)   **MAKES →** 2 DOZEN CUPCAKES

INGREDIENTS

2 cups all-purpose flour

1½ cups sugar

2½ teaspoons baking powder

1 teaspoon salt

¾ cup (1½ sticks) butter, softened

¾ cup whole milk

1½ teaspoons vanilla extract

3 large eggs

choice of frosting, pages 62–63

EACH CUPCAKE WITHOUT FROSTING

Calories: About 155

Protein: 2G

Carbohydrates: 21G

Total Fat: 7G

(Saturated Fat: 4G)

Fiber: 0G

Sodium: 210MG

1. Preheat oven to 350°F. Line twenty-four 2½-inch muffin-pan cups with paper liners.

2. In a large bowl with mixer on low speed, mix flour, sugar, baking powder, and salt until combined. Add butter, milk, vanilla, and eggs; beat just until blended. Increase speed to high; beat for 1 to 2 minutes or until creamy, occasionally scraping down sides of bowl with rubber spatula.

3. Spoon batter into prepared muffin-pan cups. Bake for 20 to 25 minutes or until cupcakes are golden brown and toothpick inserted in center of cupcakes comes out clean. Immediately remove cupcakes from pans and cool completely on wire rack.

4. When cupcakes are cool, spread frosting on tops.

SMART CHEF! If you're using a stand mixer for this recipe (or for our Rich Chocolate or Gingerbread Cupcakes, page 65 or 66), use the whisk attachment instead of the paddle attachment. Otherwise, the cupcakes will not rise properly when baked.

→ Berry-Stuffed Cupcakes

Prepare Golden Butter Cupcakes as directed, but with paring knife at an angle, cut a ¾ x 1-inch hole about halfway down center from top of each cupcake. Fill each hole with **1 teaspoon mixed berry preserves**. Mix **Vanilla Frosting**, page 62, and **1 tablespoon mixed berry preserves**. Spoon frosting into piping bag fitted with pastry tip; pipe onto cupcakes.

EACH SERVING (1 CUPCAKE): About 320 Calories, 3G Protein, 47G Carbohydrate, 13G Total Fat (7G Saturated), 1G Fiber, 187MG Sodium

?

WHAT IS IT?

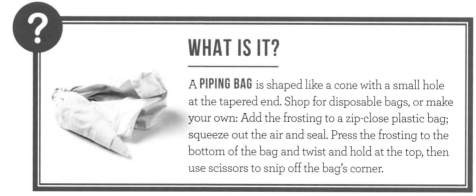

A **PIPING BAG** is shaped like a cone with a small hole at the tapered end. Shop for disposable bags, or make your own: Add the frosting to a zip-close plastic bag; squeeze out the air and seal. Press the frosting to the bottom of the bag and twist and hold at the top, then use scissors to snip off the bag's corner.

Five Fabulous
FROSTINGS

Simple to whip up and easy to spread, these frostings
are great on any of our cupcakes! All recipes make about 2 cups,
or enough to frost 2 dozen cupcakes.

→ Vanilla Frosting

In large bowl with mixer on low speed, beat **3 cups confectioners' sugar**; **½ cup butter (1 stick), softened**; **2 teaspoons vanilla extract**; and **5 tablespoons milk** until blended. Increase speed to medium-high; beat until light and fluffy, occasionally scraping down sides of bowl with rubber spatula. Beat in an additional **1 tablespoon milk**, if needed, for desired spreading consistency.

EACH TABLESPOON: About 70 Calories, 0G Protein, 11G Carbohydrate, 3G Total Fat (1G Saturated), 0G Fiber, 40MG Sodium

→ Chocolate Frosting

In large bowl with mixer on low speed, beat **4 ounces semisweet chocolate**, melted and slightly cooled; **1 ounce unsweetened chocolate**, melted and slightly cooled; and **½ cup butter (1 stick)**, softened, until blended. Add **1½ cups confectioners' sugar**, **1½ teaspoons vanilla extract**, and **3 tablespoons milk**; beat until smooth. Increase speed to medium-high; beat until light and fluffy, occasionally scraping down sides of bowl with rubber spatula. Beat in **1 tablespoon milk**, if needed, for desired spreading consistency.

EACH TABLESPOON: About 70 Calories, 0G Protein, 8G Carbohydrate, 5G Total Fat (2G Saturated), 0G Fiber, 40MG Sodium

Malted-Milk Frosting

Prepare **Chocolate Frosting**, left, as directed, but beat in **2 tablespoons malted-milk powder** with confectioners' sugar. Coarsely chop **½ cup malted-milk-ball candies**; sprinkle over frosted cupcakes.

EACH TABLESPOON: About 90 Calories, 0G Protein, 11G Carbohydrate, 6G Total Fat (3G Saturated), 0G Fiber, 54MG Sodium

Cream Cheese Frosting

In large bowl with mixer on low speed, beat **2 cups confectioners' sugar**; **4 tablespoons butter**, softened; **1 package (8 ounces) cream cheese**, softened; and **2 teaspoons vanilla extract** until blended. Increase speed to medium-high; beat until frosting is smooth and creamy, frequently scraping down sides of bowl with rubber spatula.

EACH TABLESPOON: About 55 Calories, 0G Protein, 6G Carbohydrate, 3G Total Fat (2G Saturated), 0G Fiber, 30MG Sodium

Lemony Cream Cheese Frosting

Prepare **Cream Cheese Frosting**, above, as directed, but substitute **1½ teaspoons freshly grated lemon peel** for vanilla extract.

EACH TABLESPOON: About 55 Calories, 0G Protein, 6G Carbohydrate, 3G Total Fat (2G Saturated), 0G Fiber, 30MG Sodium

SMART CHEF! Cocoa may contain stubborn clumps, so to mix it thoroughly, we use a method called *sifting*. (See Baker's Lingo, page 18.) To sift, place a fine-mesh strainer over a large bowl and add the dry ingredients to the strainer. With one hand, hold the handle of the strainer. With your other hand, gently tap the strainer until all the ingredients are strained into the bowl. Voilà—no lumps!

Rich Chocolate
CUPCAKES

Cocoa makes these cupcakes extra-fudgy. Topped with our Vanilla or
Cream Cheese Frosting, pages 62–63, they're the perfect treat for a picnic or barbecue.

ACTIVE TIME → 15 MINUTES   TOTAL TIME → 50 MINUTES (PLUS COOLING)   MAKES → 2 DOZEN CUPCAKES

INGREDIENTS

1⅓ cups all-purpose flour
⅔ cup unsweetened cocoa
1½ teaspoons baking
  powder
½ teaspoon baking soda
½ teaspoon salt
1 cup whole milk
1½ teaspoons vanilla
  extract
1⅓ cups sugar
10 tablespoons (1¼ sticks)
  butter, softened
2 large eggs
choice of frosting,
  pages 62–63

EACH CUPCAKE
WITHOUT FROSTING

Calories: About 130
Protein: 2G
Carbohydrates: 18G
Total Fat: 6G
(Saturated Fat: 4G)
Fiber: 1G
Sodium: 160MG

1. Preheat oven to 350°F. Line twenty-four 2½-inch muffin-pan cups with paper liners.

2. In medium bowl with wire whisk, mix flour, cocoa, baking powder, baking soda, and salt. In 2-cup liquid measuring cup, mix milk and vanilla.

3. In large bowl with mixer on low speed, beat sugar and butter just until blended. Increase speed to high; beat for 3 minutes or until mixture is light and creamy. Reduce speed to low; add eggs, 1 at a time, beating well after each addition.

4. Add flour mixture, alternately with milk mixture, beginning and ending with flour mixture, just until combined, occasionally scraping down sides of bowl with rubber spatula.

5. Spoon batter into prepared muffin-pan cups, filling each cup about ⅔ full. Bake for 22 to 25 minutes or until toothpick inserted in center of cupcakes comes out clean. Immediately remove cupcakes from pans and cool completely on wire rack.

6. When cupcakes are cool, spread frosting on top.

Gingerbread
CUPCAKES

Fragrant with molasses and spice, these moist cupcakes are especially delicious topped with our Lemony Cream Cheese Frosting, page 63. Gingerbread may be the most popular during Christmas, but these cupcakes will steal the show year-round.

ACTIVE TIME → 25 MINUTES   **TOTAL TIME →** 50 MINUTES (PLUS COOLING)   **MAKES →** 2 DOZEN CUPCAKES

INGREDIENTS

3 cups all-purpose flour
¾ cup sugar
1 tablespoon ground ginger
1½ teaspoons ground cinnamon
¾ teaspoon baking soda
¾ teaspoon salt
1 cup light (mild) molasses
½ cup (1 stick) butter, softened
2 large eggs
choice of frosting, pages 62–63
Pineapple Flowers, opposite, optional

EACH CUPCAKE WITHOUT FROSTING OR GARNISH

Calories: About 155
Protein: 2G
Carbohydrates: 27G
Total Fat: 4G
(Saturated Fat: 1G)
Fiber: 1G
Sodium: 175MG

1. Preheat oven to 350°F. Line twenty-four 2½-inch muffin-pan cups with paper liners.

2. In large bowl with mixer on low speed, combine flour, sugar, ginger, cinnamon, baking soda, and salt. Add molasses, butter, eggs, and 1 cup water; beat until blended. Increase speed to high; beat for 1 to 2 minutes or until creamy, occasionally scraping down sides of bowl with rubber spatula.

3. Spoon batter into prepared muffin-pan cups, filling each cup about ⅔ full. Bake for 23 to 25 minutes or until toothpick inserted in center of cupcakes comes out clean. Immediately remove cupcakes from pans and cool completely on wire rack.

4. When cupcakes are cool, spread frosting on top and garnish with Pineapple Flowers, right, if using.

→ Pineapple Flowers

Preheat oven to in 225°F. Line 2 large cookie sheets with parchment paper. Peel and scoop eyes from **1 ripe pineapple**. Blot pineapple dry with paper towels, then place on paper towel on cutting board. With serrated knife, thinly slice pineapple into ¹⁄₁₆-inch rounds; blot again. Arrange slices on prepared cookie sheets. Bake for 30 minutes, then carefully turn slices over. Bake for 30 to 40 minutes longer or until very dry. After removing from the oven and letting cool until warm but not hot, place slices into cups of a muffin pan; gently press down centers to form shallow cups. Let stand until stiff. Press gently into frosting.

New York-Style CHEESECAKE

Super rich and creamy, this is the ultimate cheesecake. You'll love our Chocolate Marble Cheesecake, too.

ACTIVE TIME → 30 MINUTES   TOTAL TIME → 1 HOUR 35 MINUTES (PLUS COOLING AND CHILLING)   MAKES → 16 SERVINGS

INGREDIENTS

GRAHAM CRACKER–CRUMB CRUST

1¼ cups graham cracker crumbs (from 11 crackers)
4 tablespoons butter, melted
1 tablespoon sugar

CHEESECAKE

3 packages (8 ounces each) cream cheese, softened
¾ cup sugar
1 tablespoon all-purpose flour
1½ teaspoons vanilla extract
3 large eggs
1 large egg yolk
¼ cup milk
fresh berries, for garnish, optional

EACH SERVING

Calories: About 275
Protein: 5G
Carbohydrates: 19G
Total Fat: 20G
(Saturated Fat: 12G)
Fiber: 0G
Sodium: 230MG

1. **Prepare Graham Cracker–Crumb Crust:** Preheat oven to 375°F. In 9-inch springform pan, with fork, mix graham cracker crumbs, melted butter, and sugar until crumbs are evenly moistened. Press crumb mixture firmly into bottom and up side of prepared springform pan. Bake for 10 minutes; cool crust, in pan, on wire rack. Reduce oven temperature to 300°F.

2. **Prepare Cheesecake:** In large bowl with mixer on medium speed, beat cream cheese and sugar until smooth and fluffy. Beat in flour and vanilla until well combined. Reduce speed to low; beat in eggs and egg yolk, 1 at a time, beating well after each addition. Beat in milk just until blended.

3. Pour batter onto prepared crust. Bake for 55 to 60 minutes or until set but still slightly jiggly and moist in center, and pale gold near edge.

4. Cool cheesecake completely, in pan, on wire rack. Refrigerate overnight before serving. With small metal spatula, loosen cake from side of pan and remove springform ring. Garnish with fresh berries, if using.

→ Chocolate Marble Cheesecake

Prepare New York–Style Cheesecake as directed, but for crust, use **1¼ cups chocolate-wafer cookie crumbs** (about 24 cookies) instead of graham crackers. In small bowl, mix **2 ounces semisweet chocolate**, melted, and **1 cup cheesecake batter**. Pour plain cheesecake batter onto prepared crust. Spoon chocolate batter on top in several dollops. Using butter knife, swirl chocolate batter through plain batter.

EACH SERVING: About 290 Calories, 5G Protein, 21G Carbohydrate, 21G Total Fat (12G Saturated), 1G Fiber, 220MG Sodium

Easiest-Ever
PASTRY DOUGH

Make this flaky, delicious dough your go-to recipe for pies, quiches, croissants—and more. Follow this recipe, and the next time someone asks if you made the crust from scratch, you can honestly reply, "YES!"

TOTAL TIME → 5 MINUTES (PLUS CHILLING)   **MAKES → 1 PIECRUST**

INGREDIENTS

1¼ cups all-purpose flour
1 tablespoon sugar
½ teaspoon kosher salt
½ cup (1 stick) cold
  unsalted butter
1 tablespoon distilled
  white vinegar

EACH PIE CRUST

Calories: About 680
Protein: 8G
Carbohydrates: 61G
Total Fat: 46G
(Saturated Fat: 29G)
Fiber: 3G
Sodium: 588MG

1. In food processor with knife blade attached, pulse flour, sugar, and salt until combined. Cut butter into small cubes, then add, pulsing until coarse crumbs form.

2. Drizzle in vinegar and 1 tablespoon ice water, pulsing until dough is crumbly but holds together when squeezed. (If necessary, add another 1 to 2 teaspoons ice water, 1 teaspoon at a time.) Do not overmix.

3. Place the dough on piece of plastic wrap and shape into 1-inch-thick disk. Wrap tightly and refrigerate until firm, at least 1 hour or up to 2 days.

SMART CHEF! If you're willing to forgo the compliments of a homemade piecrust, then a store-bought crust might be the way to go. You can make these pies with two refrigerated, ready-to-use piecrusts (for a 9-inch pie), softened as the label directs.

Easy
AS PIE!

Make two batches of our Easiest-Ever Pastry Dough, page 71, pick a double-crust pie filling, and add a Pretty Pie Top, right, and you're good to go! All recipes make 8 servings.

1. For each pie, preheat oven to 400°F. Line large rimmed baking sheet with foil.

2. On floured surface, with lightly floured rolling pin, roll first batch of **Easiest-Ever Pastry Dough** into 12-inch circle. Transfer to 9-inch pie plate. Gently press dough against bottom and up side of pie plate without stretching it. Trim dough so overhang is even (about ½ inch from edge of rim). Pour your choice of filling (Mixed Berry, Rustic Plum, or True Blueberry) into crust and dot with **3 tablespoons butter**.

3. Roll out second batch of **Easiest-Ever Pastry Dough** and place it on top (see How to: Make Pretty Pie Tops for variations, page 74); crimp edges and bake on prepared baking sheet for 1 hour or until bubbling. Cool on wire rack.

Mixed-Berry Pie Filling

In large bowl, toss **2 cups each raspberries and sliced hulled strawberries, 1 cup blackberries, ¾ cup sugar, ¼ cup cornstarch, 1 tablespoon lemon juice, and ¼ teaspoon salt.**

EACH SERVING: About 305 Calories, 3G Protein, 48G Carbohydrate, 12G Total Fat (7G Saturated), 4G Fiber, 196MG Sodium

Rustic Plum Pie Filling

In large bowl, toss **3 pounds red plums,** sliced; **¾ cup sugar; ¼ cup cornstarch; 1 tablespoon lemon juice; and ¼ teaspoon salt.** See page 74 for photo.

EACH SERVING: About 340 Calories, 3G Protein, 57G Carbohydrate, 12G Total Fat (7G Saturated), 3G Fiber, 195MG Sodium

True Blueberry Pie Filling

In large bowl, toss **5 cups blueberries, ¾ cup sugar, ¼ cup cornstarch, 1 tablespoon lemon juice,** and **¼ teaspoon salt.**

EACH SERVING: About 320 Calories, 3G Protein, 53G Carbohydrate, 12G Total Fat (7G Saturated), 3G Fiber, 196MG Sodium

FUN FOOD!

How To:
MAKE PRETTY PIE TOPS

Even accomplished bakers fret over perfecting their pie tops. Master this method for making these buttery trimmings at home. No special pastry skills required!

RUSTIC PLUM
PIE • PAGE 73

→ Lattice-Top Pie

Roll the second batch of your Easiest-Ever Pastry Dough to ⅛ inch thickness; cut into 1-inch-wide strips using a knife or a pastry wheel.

Moisten edge of bottom crust with water so that the strips stick. Place half of pastry strips across top of pie, about ¾ inch apart.

Fold every other strip halfway back. Put 1 new strip of crust across center, perpendicular to the folded strips. Unfold the folded strips.

Fold back alternate strips; place another strip across, parallel to the first. Repeat.

→ Cutout-Top Pie

Roll the second batch of your Easiest-Ever Pastry Dough to ⅛ inch thickness; stamp out shapes from the piecrust using a cookie cutter. Reroll the scraps; cut out more shapes.

Layer the dough shapes over the filling in a pattern of your choice, slightly overlapping one another if you like (brush with water to make them stick together).

HOW TO: CRIMP A PIECRUST

A properly crimped pie edge not only decorates your pie, it helps keep the filling from overflowing. Here's the secret:

1. Take the pastry overhang and roll it under itself, so you have a rolled cylinder that rests on the rim of the pie plate.

2. With one hand on the inside of the pastry edge, and one hand on the outside, use the index finger of your inside hand to push the dough between the thumb and the index finger of your outside hand to form a *U* or a *V* shape.

3. Continue the same motion all around the pie plate, spacing your indents about 1 inch apart.

75

Peachy Pecan
CRUMB PIE

Ripe peaches are a must for this recipe. Look for fruit with a pleasingly sweet fragrance and that's soft to the touch but not mushy.

ACTIVE TIME → 35 MINUTES   **TOTAL TIME →** 1 HOUR 35 MINUTES (PLUS CHILLING AND COOLING)   **MAKES →** 8 SERVINGS

INGREDIENTS
Easiest-Ever Pastry Dough, page 71

CRUMB TOPPING
½ cup all-purpose flour
¼ cup rolled oats, uncooked
¼ cup packed brown sugar
¼ cup chopped pecans
½ teaspoon freshly grated lemon peel
⅛ teaspoon salt
3 tablespoons butter, softened

FILLING
2 pounds ripe peaches (about 7 to 8 large), peeled and chopped
½ cup packed brown sugar
2 tablespoons cornstarch
¼ teaspoon ground cinnamon
1 tablespoon lemon juice
vanilla ice cream, for serving

1. Prepare Pie Shell: On lightly floured surface with lightly floured rolling pin, roll dough out into 13-inch circle. Transfer to 9-inch pie plate. Gently press dough against bottom and up side of plate without stretching it. If necessary, trim dough so overhang is even (about ½ inch from edge of rim). Fold overhang under itself and crimp as desired. Refrigerate pie shell for 30 minutes.

2. Prepare Crumb Topping: Meanwhile, place foil-lined, rimmed baking sheet in oven and preheat to 425°F. In medium bowl, with your hands, combine flour, oats, brown sugar, pecans, lemon peel, and salt. Add butter and squeeze to form small clumps. Refrigerate until ready to use.

HOW TO: PEEL A PEACH

It's easy as 1-2-3.

1. Cut a small *X* in bottom of peach with paring knife.

2. Place peach in small saucepan of boiling water for about 60 seconds.

3. With slotted spoon, transfer peach to bowl filled with ice water. When peach is cool enough to handle, slip off softened skin.

EACH SERVING

Calories: About 410
Protein: 7G
Carbohydrates: 57G
Total Fat: 19G
(Saturated Fat: 10G)
Fiber: 3G
Sodium: 199MG

3. **Prepare Filling:** Reduce oven temperature to 375°F. In large bowl, combine peaches, brown sugar, cornstarch, cinnamon, and lemon juice. Add to chilled pie shell, spreading in even layer. Take preheated baking sheet out of oven, place your pie on it, return it to oven, and bake for 35 minutes. Sprinkle crumb topping over filling. Bake for 25 to 30 minutes longer or until filling is bubbling and crust is golden brown.

4. Cool pie on wire rack. Serve warm or at room temperature with vanilla ice cream, if desired.

SMART CHEF! Make dessert early so your pie cools completely (at least two hours at room temperature); that way, when you slice into it, the filling won't run.

SMART CHEF! Use a swivel-bladed vegetable peeler on a hunk of warm, room-temperature chocolate to make gorgeous curls.

Black-Bottom
CHOCOLATE CREAM PIE

This pie takes chocolate to a whole new level! Put chocolate pudding in a chocolate cookie crust, then slather the top with whipped cream and chocolate curls. Welcome to pie heaven!

ACTIVE TIME ➜ 45 MINUTES   TOTAL TIME ➜ 55 MINUTES (PLUS COOLING AND CHILLING)   **MAKES ➜ 12 SERVINGS**

INGREDIENTS

1¼ fine chocolate wafer crumbs (about 24 wafer cookies, pulsed in food processor with knife blade attached)

6 tablespoons butter

1 cup plus 3 tablespoons sugar

⅓ cup cornstarch

¼ teaspoon salt

3½ cups whole milk

4 large egg yolks

3 ounces unsweetened chocolate, finely chopped

1 cup heavy cream

semisweet chocolate curls, for garnish

EACH SERVING

Calories: About 365
Protein: 5G
Carbohydrates: 39G
Total Fat: 22G
(Saturated Fat: 13G)
Fiber: 2G
Sodium: 185MG

1. Preheat oven to 375°F. In the microwave, melt 4 tablespoons butter in, microwave-safe bowl; add wafer crumbs and 1 tablespoon sugar. Stir until moistened. Firmly press mixture into bottom and up side of 9-inch pie plate. Bake for 10 to 12 minutes or until set. Cool crust completely on wire rack.

2. In heavy 3-quart saucepan with wire whisk, mix cornstarch, salt, and 1 cup sugar. While whisking, gradually add milk until blended. Cook over medium-high heat for 7 to 8 minutes or until boiling and thickened, whisking constantly. Remove saucepan from heat.

3. In large bowl with wire whisk, beat egg yolks until blended. Whisk in hot milk mixture in steady stream. Return mixture to saucepan and cook over medium heat for 4 to 6 minutes or until mixture boils and thickens, stirring constantly. Remove saucepan from heat and add chocolate. Stir until melted, then stir in remaining 2 tablespoons butter until melted.

4. Pour filling into cooled piecrust and spread evenly. Press sheet of plastic wrap directly against surface. Refrigerate at least 4 hours or up to overnight, or until cold and stiff.

5. In large bowl with mixer on medium-high speed, beat cream until thickened. While beating, gradually add remaining 2 tablespoons sugar. Beat until soft peaks form. Dollop over pie. Garnish with chocolate curls, if using.

Quiche
4 WAYS

Made-from-scratch quiche is a standout savory pie,
and we've raised the bar with four delicious flavor variations.

ACTIVE TIME → **25 MINUTES**   **TOTAL TIME** → **1 HOUR 25 MINUTES** (PLUS COOLING)   **MAKES** → **6 SERVINGS**

INGREDIENTS

PIECRUST

1 refrigerated ready-to-use
piecrust (for a 9-inch pie),
softened as the
label directs

CUSTARD

4 large eggs
1¼ cups whole milk
½ teaspoon salt
choice of filling

1. Preheat oven to 375°F.

2. Prepare Pie Shell: Line 1 (9-inch) pie plate with piecrust. Gently press dough against bottom and up side of pie plate without stretching it. Fold overhang under itself and crimp as desired. Line crust with parchment paper or foil and fill with pie weights or dried beans. Bake for 15 minutes or until beginning to set. Remove liner and weights. Bake for 10 to 13 minutes longer or until edge is golden and bottom is baked through. Cool crust on wire rack while you prepare Custard. Keep oven on.

3. Prepare Custard: In large bowl with wire whisk, beat eggs, milk, and salt. Stir in flavor variation of choice. Pour into cooled pie shell. Bake for 35 to 45 minutes or until center is just set. Cool quiche on wire rack for 15 minutes. Serve warm or at room temperature.

Asparagus & Bacon Quiche Filling

In 12-inch skillet, cook **6 slices thick-cut bacon**, chopped, over medium-high heat for 8 minutes or until crisp, stirring occasionally. With slotted spoon, transfer bacon to paper towel–lined plate. To same skillet, add **8 ounces asparagus**, sliced on an angle. Cook for 2 minutes, stirring. Cool slightly; stir bacon, asparagus, and **1 cup shredded Gruyère cheese** into custard.

EACH SERVING: About 350 Calories, 17G Protein, 20G Carbohydrate, 23G Total Fat (10G Saturated), 1G Fiber, 830MG Sodium

Ham & Spinach Quiche Filling

In 12-inch skillet, heat **1 tablespoon olive oil** over medium-high heat. Add **1 medium onion**, thinly sliced, and **¼ teaspoon black pepper**. Cook for 5 minutes or until the onion starts to brown. Reduce heat to medium-low; add 2 tablespoons water. Cover and cook for 10 minutes, stirring occasionally. Stir in **½ (6-ounce) bag baby spinach**. Cook for 2 minutes or just until wilted, tossing. Cool slightly; stir into custard along with **4 ounces thick-cut deli ham**, chopped.

EACH SERVING: About 265 Calories, 11G Protein, 22G Carbohydrate, 25G Total Fat (13G Saturated), 0G Fiber, 746MG Sodium

Pimento Cheese Quiche Filling

Stir **2 cups shredded extra-sharp Cheddar cheese**; **1 jar (4 ounces) chopped pimentos**, drained; **2 green onions**, thinly sliced; **2 teaspoons hot pepper sauce**; and **1 teaspoon Worcestershire sauce** into custard.

EACH SERVING: About 365 Calories, 17G Protein, 20G Carbohydrate, 25G Total Fat (13G Saturated), 0G Fiber, 746MG Sodium

Mushroom & Zucchini Quiche Filling

In 10-inch skillet, heat **2 teaspoons olive oil** over medium-high heat. Add **8 ounces sliced mushrooms** and **2 cloves garlic**, finely chopped. Cook for 8 to 10 minutes or until browned, stirring occasionally. Cool slightly. Stir mushrooms; **1¼ cups grated zucchini**, patted very dry; **⅓ cup crumbled feta cheese**; and **¼ teaspoon black pepper** into custard.

EACH SERVING: About 260 Calories, 10G Protein, 21G Carbohydrate, 16G Total Fat (7G Saturated), 1G Fiber, 516MG Sodium

3

Quick Breads, Muffins & More

Love cake that you can snack on? We've got sweet loaves like banana, date-nut, and lemon-glazed tea bread. Or if you want to whip up a breakfast treat, we've got plenty of recipes for muffins and scones (both savory and sweet!). And last but not least, our piping-hot popovers, biscuits, and loaded cornbread offer a tasty break from ho-hum dinner rolls any night of the week.

Chocolate-Glazed
BANANA BREAD MINIS

Are the bananas that you bought last week still sitting on the counter?
Are they starting to brown? Don't throw them away! Those bananas are perfect for this recipe.

ACTIVE TIME → 15 MINUTES   TOTAL TIME → 45 MINUTES (PLUS COOLING AND STANDING)   MAKES → 6 LOAVES

INGREDIENTS

2 cups all-purpose flour
¾ teaspoon baking soda
¼ teaspoon salt
2 cups mashed very ripe
  bananas
2 teaspoons vanilla extract
½ cup (1 stick) butter,
  softened
½ cup granulated sugar
½ cup packed light brown
  sugar
2 large eggs
2 ounces semisweet
  chocolate, melted

EACH ½ LOAF

Calories: About 285
Protein: 4G
Carbohydrates: 45G
Total Fat: 10G
(Saturated Fat: 6G)
Fiber: 2G
Sodium: 203MG

1. Preheat oven to 350°F.

2. In medium bowl with wire whisk, mix flour, baking soda, and salt.
In another medium bowl, mix bananas and vanilla.

3. In large bowl with mixer on medium speed, beat butter and sugars
for 3 minutes or until fluffy. Beat in eggs, 1 at a time. Reduce speed to
low; alternately add flour mixture and banana mixture, beginning and
ending with flour mixture, just until blended, scraping down side of bowl
occasionally with rubber spatula.

4. Divide batter among 6 disposable mini (¼-pound) loaf pans. Bake for 30
to 35 minutes or until toothpick inserted in centers of breads comes out
clean. Cool breads completely in pans on wire rack.

5. Drizzle cooled breads with melted chocolate; let stand until chocolate sets.

SMART CHEF! To mash bananas with ease, place the peeled fruit
on a sheet of waxed paper and mash with the tines of a fork. You'll
need 4 medium bananas for this recipe.

Double Pumpkin
CORNBREAD WITH RED ONION

This rich skillet cornbread with cream cheese, melted butter,
and pumpkin puree is fabulous served warm and with a drizzle of honey.

ACTIVE TIME → 20 MINUTES   TOTAL TIME → 45 MINUTES   MAKES → 10 SERVINGS

INGREDIENTS

2 cups all-purpose flour

2 cups yellow cornmeal

1½ tablespoons baking
powder

1 teaspoon kosher salt

1 cup whole milk

1 package (8 ounces)
cream cheese, softened

1 (15-ounce) can pure
pumpkin

2 tablespoons honey, plus
more for serving

½ cup (1 stick) unsalted
butter (no substitutions),
melted

½ small red onion,
thinly sliced

¼ cup pepitas
(pumpkin seeds)

EACH SERVING

Calories: About 435
Protein: 8G
Carbohydrates: 55G
Total Fat: 20G
(Saturated Fat: 11G)
Fiber: 3G
Sodium: 535MG

1. Place 12-inch cast-iron skillet in oven and preheat oven to 400°F.
(Cast-iron skillets are heavy, so ask an adult for help lifting it in and
out of the oven.)

2. Meanwhile, in large bowl with wire whisk, mix flour, cornmeal, baking
powder, and salt.

3. In medium bowl with wire whisk, mix milk, cream cheese, pumpkin,
honey, and 7 tablespoons melted butter. Add to cornmeal mixture and mix
just until combined.

4. With pot holders or oven mitts, carefully remove hot skillet from oven
(ask an adult for help) and brush bottom and sides with remaining 1
tablespoon butter.

5. Pour batter into heated pan. Top evenly with onion and pepitas. Bake
for 25 to 30 minutes or until toothpick inserted in center of cornbread
comes out clean.

Cranberry-Date-Nut
BREAD

We added fresh cranberries to this classic quick bread,
and it tastes even better than the original!

ACTIVE TIME → 25 MINUTES   **TOTAL TIME → 1 HOUR 40 MINUTES** (PLUS STANDING AND COOLING)   **MAKES → 16 SERVINGS**

INGREDIENTS

1 package (10 ounces)
  chopped dates (2 cups)
6 tablespoons butter
2 cups all-purpose flour
¾ cup sugar
1 teaspoon baking powder
½ teaspoon baking soda
½ teaspoon salt
1 large egg, lightly beaten
1½ cups fresh or frozen
  cranberries, coarsely
  chopped
1 cup pecans, coarsely
  chopped

EACH SERVING

Calories: About 235
Protein: 3G
Carbohydrates: 36G
Total Fat: 10G
(Saturated Fat: 1G)
Fiber: 3G
Sodium: 200MG

1. In 2-quart saucepan, heat 1 cup water to boiling over high heat. Remove saucepan from heat; stir in dates and butter. Let stand for 30 minutes or until slightly cooled.

2. Preheat oven to 325°F. Grease 9 x 5-inch loaf pan.

3. In large bowl with wire whisk, mix flour, sugar, baking powder, baking soda, and salt. With fork, stir egg into cooled date mixture. Stir date mixture, cranberries, and pecans into flour mixture just until evenly moistened (do not overmix). Spoon batter into prepared loaf pan and spread evenly.

4. Bake for 1 hour and 15 minutes or until toothpick inserted in center of bread comes out clean. Cool bread in pan on wire rack for 10 minutes. Remove from pan and cool completely on rack. Bread can be made ahead, tightly wrapped in plastic wrap, and frozen for up to 1 month.

Lemon-Glazed
EARL GREY TEA BREAD

Freshly ground tea leaves give this bread an
earthy and wholesome flavor.

ACTIVE TIME → 15 MINUTES   TOTAL TIME → 1 HOUR 35 MINUTES (PLUS COOLING AND STANDING)   **MAKES → 12 SERVINGS**

INGREDIENTS

TEA BREAD

1½ tablespoons
  decaffeinated Earl Grey
  tea leaves
1 cup granulated sugar
1½ cups all-purpose flour
¼ teaspoon baking soda
¼ teaspoon salt
½ cup (1 stick) butter,
  softened
3 large eggs, at room
  temperature
1 teaspoon vanilla extract
½ cup sour cream

LEMON GLAZE

⅔ cup confectioners' sugar
1 teaspoon freshly grated
  lemon peel

EACH SERVING

Calories: About 250
Protein: 4G
Carbohydrates: 36G
Total Fat: 11G
(Saturated Fat: 6G)
Fiber: 1G
Sodium: 160MG

1. Preheat oven to 325°F. Grease 9 x 5-inch loaf pan and then dust with flour.

2. Prepare Tea Bread: In food processor with knife blade attached, finely grind tea leaves and granulated sugar. In medium bowl with wire whisk, mix flour, baking soda, and salt.

3. In large bowl with mixer on medium-high speed, beat butter and tea sugar until fluffy. Add eggs, 1 at a time. Beat in vanilla. Reduce speed to low. Alternately, add flour mixture and sour cream, beginning and ending with flour mixture, just until blended, occasionally scraping down sides of bowl with rubber spatula.

4. Spread batter in prepared loaf pan. Bake for 1 hour 20 minutes or until toothpick inserted in center of bread comes out clean. Cool bread in pan on wire rack for 10 minutes. Remove bread from pan; cool completely on wire rack.

5. Prepare Lemon Glaze: In small bowl with wire whisk, mix confectioners' sugar, lemon peel, and 1 tablespoon water until smooth. Drizzle over bread; let stand until glaze is set. Bread can be made ahead, wrapped tightly in plastic wrap, and stored at room temperature for up to 4 days.

FUN FOOD!

Basic
MUFFINS

This recipe is better than store-bought and a snap to prepare.
For a change of pace, fold in blueberries, lemon peel and pecans, or oats and
raisins, or top with a brown-sugar-and-cinnamon streusel.

ACTIVE TIME → 15 MINUTES   TOTAL TIME → 35 MINUTES   MAKES → 12 MUFFINS

INGREDIENTS

2½ cups all-purpose flour
½ cup sugar
1 tablespoon baking
   powder
½ teaspoon salt
1 cup milk
6 tablespoons butter,
   melted
1 teaspoon vanilla extract
1 large egg

EACH MUFFIN

Calories: About 195
Protein: 4G
Carbohydrates: 29G
Total Fat: 7G
(Saturated Fat: 2G)
Fiber: 1G
Sodium: 290MG

1. Preheat oven to 400°F. Grease twelve 2½ x 1¼-inch muffin-pan cups.
In large bowl with wire whisk, mix flour, sugar, baking powder, and salt. In
small bowl with fork, beat milk, melted butter, vanilla, and egg until well
blended. Add liquid mixture to flour mixture; stir just until flour is evenly
moistened. Spoon batter into prepared muffin-pan cups.

2. Bake for 18 to 20 minutes or until toothpick inserted in centers of muffins
comes out clean. Immediately remove muffins from pan. Serve warm, or
cool on wire rack.

Fresh Blueberry Muffins

Prepare Basic Muffins as directed, but fold **1 cup fresh blueberries** into batter before spooning batter into muffin cups.

EACH MUFFIN: About 200 Calories, 4G Protein, 31G Carbohydrate, 7G Total Fat (2G Saturated), 1G Fiber, 290MG Sodium

Lemon-Pecan Muffins

Prepare Basic Muffins as directed, but add **1½ teaspoons freshly grated lemon peel** to liquid mixture, and stir **½ cup chopped, toasted pecans** into flour mixture. While muffins are baking, prepare glaze: In small bowl, with fork, mix **¾ cup confectioners' sugar** and **2 tablespoons fresh lemon juice.** Brush glaze on hot muffins after removing from pan.

EACH MUFFIN: About 255 Calories, 4G Protein, 38G Carbohydrate, 10G Total Fat (2G Saturated), 1G Fiber, 290MG Sodium

Streusel-Topped Muffins

Prepare Basic Muffins as directed, but after spooning batter into muffin-pan cups, prepare topping. In small bowl, with your fingertips, **mix ⅓ cup all-purpose flour; ⅓ cup packed light brown sugar; 2 tablespoons butter,** softened; and **¼ teaspoon ground cinnamon** until blended. Squeeze mixture in your hands to form large crumbs. Gently press crumbs into tops of muffins before baking.

EACH MUFFIN: About 250 Calories, 4G Protein, 38G Carbohydrate, 9G Total Fat (2G Saturated), 1G Fiber, 315MG Sodium

Oatmeal-Raisin Muffins

Prepare Basic Muffins as directed, but reduce flour to 1½ cups and stir **1 cup old-fashioned or quick-cooking oats** into liquid mixture. Fold **½ cup raisins** into batter before spooning into muffin cups.

EACH MUFFIN: About 230 Calories, 5G Protein, 35G Carbohydrate, 8G Total Fat (2G Saturated), 2G Fiber, 290MG Sodium

Spiced Plum
& QUINOA MUFFINS

Quinoa (pronounced KEEN-wah) is an edible seed that's packed with protein.
If you're looking to power up the most important meal of the day, try these ultimate protein muffins.

ACTIVE TIME → 20 MINUTES   TOTAL TIME → 35 MINUTES   MAKES → 18 MUFFINS

INGREDIENTS

1¼ cups all-purpose flour
1 cup whole wheat flour
⅓ cup white quinoa,
    uncooked
1½ teaspoons baking
    powder
1 teaspoon ground
    cinnamon
½ teaspoon ground ginger
½ teaspoon baking soda
½ teaspoon salt
2 large eggs, beaten
1 cup plain full-fat yogurt
½ cup (1 stick) butter,
    melted
½ cup honey
3 plums, 1 chopped and
    2 thinly sliced

EACH MUFFIN

Calories: About 160
Protein: 4G
Carbohydrates: 23G
Total Fat: 7G
(Saturated Fat: 4G)
Fiber: 1G
Sodium: 200MG

1. Preheat oven to 400°F. Line eighteen 2½ x 1¼-inch muffin-pan cups with paper liners. In large bowl with wire whisk, mix flours, quinoa, baking powder, cinnamon, ginger, baking soda, and salt.

2. In medium bowl with wire whisk, beat eggs, yogurt, melted butter, and honey until blended. Fold egg mixture into flour mixture just until blended; stir in chopped plums. Divide batter among prepared muffin-pan cups (about ¼ cup each) and top each with a couple of plum slices.

3. Bake for 15 to 20 minutes or until toothpick inserted into centers of muffins comes out clean. Cool muffins in pans for 5 minutes. Remove muffins from pans and cool completely on wire racks.

SMART CHEF! You can swap in 2 peaches or nectarines or 1 mango for plums. Or stir ½ cup of your favorite dried fruit, chopped, into the batter.

FUN FOOD!

Classic
POPOVERS

You'll amaze friends and family with this stunning (yet surprisingly easy) recipe that includes fabulous flavor variations. If you don't have a popover pan, use eight 6- to 8-ounce ramekins—or single-portion baking dishes—and bake on a rimmed baking sheet.

ACTIVE TIME → 10 MINUTES   TOTAL TIME → 1 HOUR   MAKES → 6 POPOVERS

INGREDIENTS

3 large eggs
1 cup whole milk
1 cup all-purpose flour
3 tablespoons butter, melted, plus more for greasing the pan
½ teaspoon salt

EACH POPOVER

Calories: About 205
Protein: 7G
Carbohydrates: 18G
Total Fat: 12G
(Saturated Fat: 6G)
Fiber: 1G
Sodium: 310MG

1. Preheat oven to 375°F. Generously grease cups of popover pan.

2. In blender, puree eggs, milk, flour, butter, and salt until smooth.

3. Divide batter evenly among prepared popover cups. Bake for 40 minutes.

4. With small paring knife, cut small slit in top of each popover to let out steam. Bake for 10 minutes longer. Remove popovers from oven; immediately transfer from popover cups to wire rack. Serve warm. Cooled popovers can be made ahead and kept at room temperature for up to 3 hours or stored in zip-seal plastic bag and frozen for up to 1 month. Reheat at 350°F until crisp.

?

WHAT IS IT?

A **POPOVER PAN** features six deep, narrow cups, which force the batter in each cup to rise to its fullest height during baking. Popover pans made of dark metal produce the best crust.

Sweet Cocoa Popovers

Prepare Classic Popovers as directed, but reduce flour to ¾ cup. Blend ¼ cup unsweetened cocoa and 3 tablespoons sugar into batter.

EACH SERVING: About 210 Calories, 7G Protein, 22G Carbohydrate, 11G Total Fat (6G Saturated), 2G Fiber, 301MG Sodium

Bacon-Cheese Popovers

Prepare Classic Popovers as directed, but reduce salt to ¼ teaspoon. Blend **4 slices cooked bacon**, chopped; **½ cup shredded sharp Cheddar cheese**; and **¼ cup finely grated Parmesan cheese** into batter.

EACH SERVING: About 275 Calories, 12G Protein, 19G Carbohydrate, 17G Total Fat (9G Saturated), 1G Fiber, 412MG Sodium

Savory Spiced Popovers

Prepare Classic Popovers as directed, but blend **1½ teaspoons ground cumin**, **1 teaspoon smoked paprika**, and **¼ teaspoon black pepper** into batter.

EACH SERVING: About 205 Calories, 7G Protein, 18G Carbohydrate, 11G Total Fat (6G Saturated), 1G Fiber, 310MG Sodium

Strawberry
SHORTCAKES

There's nothing more delicious than this spring classic. For truly superb shortcakes, assemble and serve the dessert while the shortcakes are still warm.

ACTIVE TIME → 25 MINUTES   TOTAL TIME → 50 MINUTES (PLUS COOLING)   MAKES → 8 SERVINGS

INGREDIENTS
SHORTCAKES
2 cups all-purpose flour
6 tablespoons sugar
2 teaspoons baking
  powder
¼ teaspoon salt
⅓ cup cold butter, cut up
⅔ cup whole milk

STRAWBERRY FILLING
6 cups strawberries, hulled
  and halved
⅓ cup sugar
1 cup heavy cream

EACH SERVING
Calories: About 410
Protein: 5G
Carbohydrates: 53G
Total Fat: 21G
(Saturated Fat: 12G)
Fiber: 4G
Sodium: 295MG

1. **Prepare Shortcakes:** Preheat oven to 425°F. Line large cookie sheet with parchment paper. In medium bowl with wire whisk, mix flour, 3 tablespoons sugar, baking powder, and salt. With pastry blender or 2 knives used scissor-fashion, cut in butter until mixture resembles coarse crumbs. Stir in milk just until mixture forms soft dough that doesn't stick to side of bowl.

2. Transfer dough to lightly floured surface. Knead dough about 10 times, just until dough comes together. Pat into 1-inch-thick round. With floured 2½-inch round biscuit cutter, cut out 8 shortcakes without twisting cutter.

3. With wide metal spatula, carefully transfer rounds, 2 inches apart, to prepared cookie sheet, placing 2 inches apart. Sprinkle tops with 1 tablespoon sugar. Bake for 15 to 20 minutes or until bottoms are golden brown. Transfer shortcakes to wire rack to cool slightly.

4. **Prepare Strawberry Filling:** Meanwhile, in medium bowl, combine strawberries and sugar until sugar has dissolved.

5. In large bowl with mixer on medium speed, beat cream just until soft peaks form. Beat in remaining 2 tablespoons sugar.

6. To serve, slice shortcakes horizontally in half with serrated knife. Top bottom halves with strawberry filling and whipped cream. Replace tops.

Best-Ever
BUTTERMILK BISCUITS

Shortening in the dough makes these biscuits extra flaky.

ACTIVE TIME → 10 MINUTES   TOTAL TIME → 25 MINUTES   MAKES → 14 BISCUITS

INGREDIENTS

4 cups all-purpose flour

5 teaspoons baking powder

1 tablespoon sugar

1 teaspoon baking soda

¾ teaspoon salt

½ cup trans-fat-free shortening, cut up and cold

1½ cups low-fat buttermilk

3 tablespoons butter, melted

EACH BISCUIT

Calories: About 390
Protein: 4G
Carbohydrates: 29G
Total Fat: 9G
(Saturated Fat: 3G)
Fiber: 1G
Sodium: 410MG

1. Preheat oven to 450°F. Line large cookie sheet with parchment paper. In food processor with knife blade attached, pulse flour, baking powder, sugar, baking soda, and salt until combined. Add shortening; pulse just until coarse crumbs form. Transfer flour mixture to large bowl. Stir in buttermilk just until dough starts to come together.

2. Transfer dough to lightly floured surface; knead just until smooth, 6 to 8 times. With floured rolling pin, roll dough to ½-inch thickness. With floured 2½-inch round biscuit cutter, cut out as many rounds as possible without twisting cutter. With spatula, carefully transfer the rounds to prepared cookie sheet, placing 1 inch apart.

3. Gently press scraps together. Reroll and cut once more for total of 14 biscuits. Brush tops with melted butter. Bake for 12 to 15 minutes or until golden brown. Serve warm.

SMART CHEF! To chill the shortening quickly, scoop it from the measuring cup onto a sheet of waxed paper and freeze for 10 minutes.

Fluffy
APPLE-CHEDDAR BISCUITS

These deluxe biscuits are studded with chopped Granny Smith apple and shredded extra-sharp Cheddar cheese. With all these flavors happening at once, it's a party in your mouth!

ACTIVE TIME → 25 MINUTES   TOTAL TIME → 50 MINUTES   MAKES → 16 BISCUITS

INGREDIENTS

3 cups all-purpose flour

3 tablespoons sugar

1 tablespoon plus ½ teaspoon baking powder

½ teaspoon salt

¾ cup peeled, finely chopped Granny Smith apple

3 ounces (¾ cup) shredded extra-sharp Cheddar cheese

10 tablespoons butter, frozen and coarsely grated

2 green onions, thinly sliced

½ teaspoon black pepper

¾ cup whole milk

1 large egg, beaten

EACH BISCUIT

Calories: About 195
Protein: 5G
Carbohydrates: 22G
Total Fat: 10G
(Saturated Fat: 6G)
Fiber: 1G
Sodium: 285MG

1. Preheat oven to 400°F. Line large cookie sheet with parchment paper.

2. In large bowl with wire whisk, mix flour, sugar, baking powder, and salt. Stir in apple, Cheddar, butter, green onions, and black pepper. Using your stirring utensil, push the mixture up against the sides of the bowl until there is a bowl shape, or a *well*, in the center. Add milk and egg; slowly stir together until just combined but not fully blended.

3. Transfer dough to lightly floured surface; gently knead until dough just comes together. Gently pat into 1-inch-thick square. With floured chef's knife, cut dough into 16 squares. With spatula, place squares, 1 inch apart, on prepared cookie sheet. Bake for 15 to 20 minutes or until bottoms are deep golden brown. Serve warm. Cooled biscuits can be made ahead, placed in airtight container, and stored at room temperature for up to 2 days. Just before serving, reheat in 425°F oven for 8 minutes or until hot.

?

WHAT IS IT?

A **BISCUIT CUTTER** is a metal ring with a handle used for cutting out biscuit dough. Taller than a cookie cutter, its ring should have a sharp edge, so you don't have to twist. (Twisting can pinch biscuit dough, preventing the layers from separating and keeping the biscuits from rising as high when baked.)

Sesame
BISCUITS

These fancy biscuits, coated with fragrant sesame seeds, are the perfect accompaniment to your favorite soup or stew. This recipe makes 16 biscuits, so you'll have plenty of extras to freeze for other meals.

ACTIVE TIME → 15 MINUTES   TOTAL TIME → 30 MINUTES   MAKES → 16 BISCUITS

INGREDIENTS

3 cups self-rising flour,
  plus more for dusting
6 tablespoons cold butter
  (no substitutions), cut up
½ teaspoon salt
1½ cups low-fat buttermilk
1 large egg, lightly beaten
¼ cup sesame seeds

EACH BISCUIT

Calories: About 155
Protein: 5G
Carbohydrates: 22G
Total Fat: 6G
(Saturated Fat: 3G)
Fiber: 1G
Sodium: 450MG

1. Preheat oven to 450°F.

2. In large bowl with wire whisk, mix flour, butter, and salt. With pastry blender or 2 knives used scissors-fashion, cut butter into flour until mixture resembles coarse crumbs. Stir in buttermilk; with rubber spatula, mix until dough just comes together.

3. Transfer dough onto well-floured surface. Fold and gently knead dough just until no longer sticky. Pat into 7-inch square. With a floured chef's knife, cut crosswise into 4 strips, then lengthwise to form 16 cubes. Lightly brush tops with beaten egg.

4. Place sesame seeds in shallow dish or pie plate. Working 1 at a time, press each biscuit, egg side down, into seeds. Place biscuit, seed side up, on large ungreased cookie sheet. Repeat with remaining biscuits, spacing about 1 inch apart. Bake for 14 to 16 minutes or until golden brown. Cooled biscuits can be made ahead, stored in zip-seal plastic bag, and frozen for up to 2 weeks. To reheat, bake on cookie sheet in 400°F oven for 13 to 14 minutes.

Simple
SCONES

These mix-and-match scones will brighten any morning.
If you can't decide which one to try, just try them all!

ACTIVE TIME → 15 MINUTES   TOTAL TIME → 35 MINUTES (PLUS COOLING)   **MAKES → 6 SCONES**

INGREDIENTS

2 cups all-purpose flour
¼ cup sugar, optional
2½ teaspoons baking
   powder
¼ teaspoon salt
6 tablespoons cold butter,
   cut up
½ cup whole milk
1 large egg, lightly beaten
choice of mix-ins

1. Preheat oven to 400°F. Line medium cookie sheet with parchment paper.

2. In food processor with knife blade attached, pulse flour, sugar (if using), baking powder, and salt. Add butter; pulse until coarse crumbs form. Transfer flour mixture to large bowl. Using your stirring utensil, push the mixture up against the sides of the bowl until there is a well in the center. To well, add milk, egg, and your choice of mix-in.

3. With rubber spatula, stir milk mixture into flour until combined. With your hands, gently knead dough just until it starts to come together. Transfer dough to floured work surface; pat into 8 x 4-inch rectangle. Cut into six 4-inch-long rectangles. With wide spatula, transfer scones to prepared cookie sheet. Bake for 20 to 22 minutes or until golden brown. Cool in pan on wire rack. Serve warm or at room temperature. Scones can be made ahead, wrapped tightly in foil, and refrigerated for up to 3 days or frozen for up to 1 month. Reheat in 375°F oven for 8 to 10 minutes.

Lemon-Apricot Scones

Prepare Simple Scones with sugar as directed. Mix in **1 cup dried apricots**, chopped, and **1 teaspoon freshly grated lemon peel**.

EACH SCONE: About 380 Calories, 7G Protein, 59G Carbohydrate, 14G Total Fat (8G Saturated), 1G Fiber, 450MG Sodium

Raspberry-White Chocolate Scones

Prepare Simple Scones with sugar as directed. Mix in **1½ cups (6 ounces) raspberries** and **1 teaspoon vanilla extract**. Drizzle baked scones with **3 ounces melted white chocolate**.

EACH SCONE: About 410 Calories, 7G Protein, 54G Carbohydrate, 18G Total Fat (11G Saturated), 3G Fiber, 460MG Sodium

Parmesan-Herb Scones

Prepare Simple Scones as directed but omit sugar. Mix in **3 tablespoons chopped fresh dill**, **2 tablespoons chopped fresh flat-leaf parsley leaves**, **2 tablespoons chopped fresh tarragon leaves**, **⅓ cup finely grated Parmesan cheese**, and additional **¼ teaspoon salt**.

EACH SCONE: About 305 Calories, 8G Protein, 34G Carbohydrate, 15G Total Fat (9G Saturated), 1G Fiber, 615MG Sodium

Bacon-Green Onion Scones

Prepare Simple Scones as directed but omit sugar. Mix in **5 slices cooked bacon**, crumbled; **3 green onions**, finely chopped; and additional **¼ teaspoon salt**.

EACH SCONE: About 320 Calories, 9G Protein, 35G Carbohydrate, 16G Total Fat (9G Saturated), 1G Fiber, 660MG Sodium

4

Pizza Plus

Why order when you can make your own Classic Margherita Pizza,
Spicy Sausage & Cheese Pizza, Zucchini-Pesto Pizza, or BBQ Chicken Pizza?
If you're looking for something simpler, try our specialty toppers to dress up any
frozen pizza, or try our Cookie "Pizza" if your sweet tooth is calling. Our Pizza-Tastic
Dough recipe is so flexible, it can be used for pies, bagels, and
cinnamon rolls—all of which are included in this chapter!

Pizza-Tastic
DOUGH

From the ultimate pizza crust to bagels to cinnamon rolls and more, our foolproof dough can rise to any occasion.

TOTAL TIME → **10 MINUTES** (PLUS CHILLING AND STANDING)   **MAKES** → **1 POUND DOUGH**

INGREDIENTS

3 cups all-purpose flour
1 tablespoon sugar
1 teaspoon instant yeast
1 tablespoon plus 2 teaspoons olive oil
1 teaspoon salt

1. In food processor with knife blade attached, pulse flour, sugar, and yeast. With machine running, drizzle in 1 cup plus 2 tablespoons warm water (105–115°F) until combined. Add 1 tablespoon olive oil and salt. Process until dough forms a ball; transfer to lightly oiled large bowl.

2. With lightly oiled hands, knead dough for 1 minute. Form into ball; drizzle with remaining 2 teaspoons olive oil, rubbing to coat surface. Cover dough tightly with plastic wrap and refrigerate for at least 1 day or for up to 3 days. Let stand at room temperature for 1 hour before using.

SMART CHEF! Supermarkets and local pizzarias sell dough, so if you want your pizza now, buy a ball or two.

Skillet Pizza

Preheat oven to 425°F. Brush bottom and side of 12-inch cast-iron skillet with **2 teaspoons olive oil**. (Cast-iron skillets are heavy, so ask an adult for help lifting it in and out of the oven!) Press and stretch **Pizza-Tastic Dough** to 12-inch round; place in skillet. Spread with ¼ **cup marinara sauce**; top with **4 ounces fresh mozzarella cheese**, thinly sliced, and ¼ **cup pepperoni slices**. Dollop with **3 tablespoons store-bought refrigerated pesto**. Cook pizza over medium-high heat on stovetop for 3 minutes or until bottom starts to set. Place pizza in oven; bake for 20 minutes or until deep golden brown. Serve topped with **handful of arugula** and **drizzle of balsamic vinegar**. Serves 6.

EACH SERVING: About 405 Calories, 12G Protein, 52G Carbohydrate, 16G Total Fat (5G Saturated), 2G Fiber, 571MG Sodium

"Everything" Bagels

Preheat oven to 425°F. Line large rimmed baking sheet with parchment paper. In shallow dish, mix **3 tablespoons each sesame seeds, poppy seeds, and dried onion flakes**, and **1 tablespoon coarse salt**. For each bagel, roll **4 ounces Pizza-Tastic Dough** into 10-inch rope, then pinch ends together to form ring. In large pot of boiling water, cook dough rings for 2 minutes, turning over occasionally. With slotted spoon, transfer rings to dish with seed mixture and turn to coat, then place them on prepared baking sheet. Bake for 25 minutes or until deep golden brown. Serve warm or toasted. Serves 5.

EACH SERVING: About 475 Calories, 12G Protein, 80G Carbohydrate, 11G Total Fat (2G Saturated), 5G Fiber, 1,739MG Sodium

Glazed Cinnamon Rolls

Preheat oven to 425°F. Grease 8 x 8-inch metal baking pan. With lightly floured rolling pin, roll **Pizza-Tastic Dough** to 15 x 12-inch rectangle. Spread with **3 tablespoons butter**, softened; sprinkle with ¼ **cup light brown sugar** and **1 teaspoon ground cinnamon**. Roll tightly from long side to form log. Cut into 9 even pieces; place in pan, cut sides up. Dollop top of each cinnamon roll with ½ **teaspoon softened butter**. Cover with foil and bake for 20 minutes. Uncover and bake for 15 to 20 minutes longer or until tops are golden brown. For glaze, mix **1 cup confectioners' sugar**, **2 tablespoons milk**, and **pinch salt** until smooth. When rolls have cooled slightly, drizzle with glaze. Serve warm. Serves 9.

EACH SERVING: About 310 Calories, 5G Protein, 53G Carbohydrate, 9G Total Fat (4G Saturated), 1G Fiber, 324MG Sodium

Classic
MARGHERITA PIZZA

What's better than a classic margherita pizza? A margherita pizza that comes
with a tasty variation! Go for the Arugula Salad Pizza if you're craving something fresh and light.

ACTIVE TIME → 15 MINUTES   TOTAL TIME → 30 MINUTES   MAKES → 4 SERVINGS

INGREDIENTS

Pizza-Tastic Dough, page
  106
¾ cup marinara sauce
6 ounces fresh mozzarella
  cheese, thinly sliced
¼ cup grated Parmesan
  cheese
¼ cup packed fresh basil,
  sliced

EACH SERVING

Calories: About 575
Protein: 20G
Carbohydrates: 80G
Total Fat: 19G
(Saturated Fat: 8G)
Fiber: 4G
Sodium: 914MG

1. Place large cookie sheet in oven. Preheat oven to 475°F.

2. Stretch dough into small circle. Place dough on large sheet of parchment paper, stretching and pressing to form 14-inch circle with slight rim. Spread sauce on dough; top evenly with mozzarella. Remove hot cookie sheet from oven. Carefully slide parchment with dough onto hot cookie sheet (ask an adult if you need help).

3. Sprinkle pizza with Parmesan. Place pizza in oven; bake for 15 to 20 minutes or until bottom is crisp and golden brown. Top with basil.

→ Arugula Salad Pizza

Prepare Classic Margherita Pizza as directed, but stretch dough into 15 x 10–inch rectangle and omit basil. Meanwhile, in large bowl, whisk **2 tablespoons fresh lemon juice, 1 tablespoon extra-virgin olive oil, 1 teaspoon honey, and ⅛ teaspoon each salt and black pepper.** Add **1 (5-ounce) bag baby arugula and ¼ cup packed fresh basil leaves,** torn; toss until well coated. Cut pizza into quarters. Top with salad, **2 ounces prosciutto slices,** torn into ribbons, and **1 ounce shaved Parmesan cheese.** Serves 4.

EACH SERVING: About 680 Calories, 27G Protein, 84G Carbohydrate, 27G Total Fat (10G Saturated), 3G Fiber, 1,455MG Sodium

Pizza
PRIMAVERA

This springtime pizza has a simple topping of asparagus, red onion, and fontina cheese. If you want to splurge on taste, use Italian fontina.

ACTIVE TIME → 15 MINUTES   TOTAL TIME → 40 MINUTES   MAKES → 4 SERVINGS

INGREDIENTS

1 bunch asparagus, trimmed and thinly sliced on an angle

½ small red onion, very thinly sliced

2 tablespoons olive oil

½ teaspoon ground black pepper

Pizza-Tastic Dough, page 106

4 ounces (1 cup) shredded fontina cheese

EACH SERVING

Calories: About 590
Protein: 19G
Carbohydrates: 78G
Total Fat: 22G
(Saturated Fat: 7G)
Fiber: 4G
Sodium: 817MG

1. Place large cookie sheet in oven. Preheat oven to 475°F. Meanwhile, in large bowl, combine asparagus, onion, oil, and pepper, tossing to coat.

2. Stretch dough round into small circle. Place dough on large sheet of parchment paper, stretching to form 12-inch circle with slight rim. Sprinkle fontina evenly on dough. Then sprinkle asparagus mixture on top of cheese.

3. Remove hot cookie sheet from oven. Carefully slide parchment with dough onto hot cookie sheet (ask an adult if you need help). Place pizza in oven; bake for 20 to 25 minutes or until bottom and edges are deep golden brown.

HOW TO: SHAPE PIZZA DOUGH

To stretch pizza dough into a circle with a slightly raised edge, follow these simple steps:

1. On a floured surface with floured fingertips, press the dough into a flat disk.

2. Working from the center, push the dough outward with fingers spread, making the disk larger. If it pulls back, let rest 5 minutes and try again.

3. Pick up the dough. Move your hands along the edges, allowing gravity to pull the dough into your desired shape. If the dough becomes too thin while stretching, return it to the surface and pull and stretch from there.

Frozen
FIXES

Easy add-ons take a 12-inch frozen cheese pizza from tired to inspired.
Just pick a topping below and bake as the label directs (except where noted).

→ ¼ cup thinly sliced roasted peppers and ⅓ cup Kalamata olives, pitted and chopped

→ 1½ cups sliced mushrooms; 2 garlic cloves, thinly sliced; and 1 teaspoon fresh thyme leaves, chopped

→ ⅓ cup chopped ham and 6 fresh sage leaves, torn

→ ⅓ cup chopped walnuts, ¼ cup crumbled blue cheese, and ⅛ teaspoon black pepper

→ 4 slices cooked bacon, crumbled; ½ teaspoon crushed red pepper; and 2 teaspoons snipped fresh chives

→ 8 ounces frozen (thawed) shelled and deveined shrimp; 1 garlic clove, crushed in press; 1 tablespoon chopped fresh parsley; and 1 teaspoon freshly grated lemon peel

→ ½ cup ricotta cheese and ¼ cup store-bought refrigerated pesto

→ ½ bunch asparagus, trimmed and chopped; top with 3 fried eggs after baking

→ 3 tablespoons grated Parmesan cheese and 8 fresh basil leaves

FUN FOOD!

Fruit FOCACCIA

This sweet version of the classic Italian bread is topped with fresh blueberries and raspberries. If you're looking for something fresh and not too sweet, you've come to the right place.

ACTIVE TIME → **20 MINUTES**   **TOTAL TIME** → **40 MINUTES** (PLUS STANDING AND COOLING)   **MAKES** → **8 SERVINGS**

INGREDIENTS

Pizza-Tastic Dough, page 106
1 tablespoon olive oil
2 teaspoons butter, melted
4 tablespoons granulated sugar
1 cup blueberries
1 cup raspberries
confectioners' sugar, for dusting

EACH SERVING

Calories: About 280
Protein: 5G
Carbohydrates: 51G
Total Fat: 6G
(Saturated Fat: 1G)
Fiber: 3G
Sodium: 300MG

1. Preheat oven to 425°F. Line 15½ x 10½-inch rimmed baking sheet with parchment paper.

2. On lightly floured surface with floured rolling pin, roll dough to 14 x 10-inch oval. Transfer to prepared baking sheet and reshape into oval, if necessary. Cover with clean kitchen towel and let stand 15 minutes.

3. In cup, mix oil and melted butter; brush over dough. Sprinkle dough with 2 tablespoons granulated sugar. Bake for 10 minutes. Remove focaccia from oven and top with blueberries and raspberries; sprinkle with remaining 2 tablespoons granulated sugar. Bake 10 to 15 minutes longer or until fruit is juicy and crust is browned at edges.

4. Slide focaccia with parchment paper onto wire rack. Loosen bottom of focaccia with metal spatula and remove parchment paper. Cool slightly to serve warm, or serve at room temperature. To serve, sprinkle focaccia lightly with confectioners' sugar.

Spicy Sausage
& CHEESE PIZZA

Using a prebaked pizza crust takes the guesswork out of making a great pie.
Try this recipe with chorizo sausage, or check out our other variations.

ACTIVE TIME → 10 MINUTES   **TOTAL TIME** → 30 MINUTES   **MAKES** → 4 SERVINGS

INGREDIENTS

1 teaspoon olive oil

1 large (12-inch) store-bought, prebaked thin pizza crust

½ cup marinara sauce

½ cup finely chopped fully cooked chorizo sausage

4 ounces (1 cup) shredded Manchego (or mozzarella) cheese

½ cup roasted red peppers, thinly sliced

½ small red onion, thinly sliced

3 tablespoons finely chopped fresh parsley, for garnish

EACH SERVING

Calories: About 445
Protein: 19G
Carbohydrates: 41G
Total Fat: 22G
(Saturated Fat: 10G)
Fiber: 3G
Sodium: 990MG

1. Preheat oven to 425°F. Brush large cookie sheet with oil. Place crust on prepared cookie sheet.

2. Spread marinara sauce on crust in even layer. Top evenly with sausage, cheese, roasted peppers, and onion.

3. Bake for 15 to 20 minutes or until crust is golden brown and cheese has melted. Garnish with parsley.

→ Crispy Kale White Pizza

Prepare Spicy Sausage & Cheese Pizza as directed through step 1. In medium bowl, mix **1 cup part-skim ricotta cheese**; **⅓ cup grated Parmesan cheese**; **1 can (4 ounces) chopped green chilies**; **1 garlic clove**, crushed in press; **½ teaspoon dried oregano**; and **¼ teaspoon each salt and black pepper**. Spread cheese mixture on crust in even layer. Sprinkle with **1 cup shredded part-skim mozzarella cheese** and **½ teaspoon crushed red pepper**. In large bowl, toss **3 large kale leaves**, tough ribs removed and torn into bite-size pieces; **1 teaspoon oil**; and **pinch salt**. Arrange on top of cheese in single layer. Bake for 10 to 15 minutes or until crust is golden and kale is crisp. Garnish with **¼ cup chopped fresh tomato**. Serves 4.

EACH SERVING: About 465 Calories, 27G Protein, 46G Carbohydrate, 20G Total Fat (8G Saturated), 3G Fiber, 1,090MG Sodium

→ Zucchini-Pesto Pizza

Prepare Spicy Sausage & Cheese Pizza as directed through step 1. Meanwhile, seed and slice **2 small tomatoes**; place on paper towels. Sprinkle with ¼ **teaspoon salt**; let stand for 10 minutes. Spread ½ **cup store-bought refrigerated pesto** on crust. Blot tomatoes; place on pesto. Top with **8 ounces zucchini and summer squash**, thinly sliced; **2 teaspoons olive oil**; ⅓ **cup grated Pecorino cheese**; and ¼ **teaspoon black pepper**. Bake for 15 minutes or until zucchini is tender. Grate **peel of 1 small lemon** over pizza. Top with ¼ **cup packed fresh mint leaves**, chopped. Serves 4.

EACH SERVING: About 455 Calories, 16G Protein, 41G Carbohydrate, 25G Total Fat (6G Saturated), 4G Fiber, 1,005MG Sodium

More Pizza
IDEAS!

Grab a prebaked pizza crust, take your pick from our Ingredient Guide, opposite, and build your own custom pie. This is your chance to get creative and think about what ingredients YOU love best.

1. Preheat oven to 425°F. Spray large cookie sheet with nonstick cooking spray.

2. Place 1 large prebaked pizza crust on prepared cookie sheet. Spread crust with SAUCE.

3. Top with SHREDDED CHEESE, COOKED PROTEIN, if using, and TENDER VEGGIES.

4. Spray top of pizza with nonstick cooking spray. Bake for 20 to 25 minutes or until bottom is deep golden brown.

5. Top with GARNISH.

HOW TO: REHEAT PIZZA

Got leftover pizza? Forget the microwave—it just makes the crust chewy and tough. Here's the secret to enjoy a piping-hot slice (or slices) in just minutes.

ONE SLICE: Heat medium skillet over medium-high heat for 1 minute. Add 1 pizza slice, cover loosely with lid, and cook for 2 to 3 minutes.

TWO SLICES: Toast slices in toaster oven to medium darkness (two cycles if the pizza comes straight from the fridge).

THREE SLICES OR MORE: Place foil-lined cookie sheet in oven and preheat to 450°F (high heat makes the crust crispy). Place slices on hot cookie sheet and bake for 10 minutes or until cheese is bubbly.

INGREDIENT GUIDE

Mix and match one or more ingredients from each category to personalize your pizza.

1/2 CUP SAUCE

- marinara sauce
- pesto (sun-dried tomato or basil)
- olive tapenade

1 CUP SHREDDED CHEESE

- mozzarella
- Cheddar
- Gruyère
- Monterey or pepper Jack

COOKED PROTEIN, OPTIONAL

- 4 ounces chopped cooked chicken
- 2 ounces sliced pepperoni
- 2 ounces sliced prosciutto
- 2 ounces chopped cooked turkey
- 4 ounces chopped ham

2 CUPS SLICED TENDER VEGGIES

- tomatoes (plum or grape)
- mushrooms
- summer squash
- red onion
- bell pepper

GARNISH, TO TASTE

- chopped parsley
- thinly sliced basil
- snipped chives
- baby arugula

TRY THIS COMBO!
ROASTED TOMATO & CHIVE PIZZA

Prepare recipe as directed, but use ½ **cup olive tapenade** for SAUCE; **1 cup Gruyère** for SHREDDED CHEESE; **1¾ cups grape tomatoes** and **¼ cup mushrooms** for SLICED TENDER VEGGIES; and **snipped chives**, to taste, for GARNISH.

Spinach-Artichoke
PIZZA

Like deep-dish pizza—but baked in half the time—a French bread pizza holds up to hearty toppings. If you want extra flavor, swap out the French or Italian bread for garlic bread in this recipe and any of its variations.

ACTIVE TIME → 10 MINUTES   TOTAL TIME → 25 MINUTES   MAKES → 4 SERVINGS

INGREDIENTS

1 loaf soft French or Italian bread (about 12 ounces)

2 tablespoons olive oil

1¼ cups shredded part-skim mozzarella cheese

1 package (10 ounces) frozen chopped spinach, thawed and squeezed dry

1 package (8 ounces) reduced-fat cream cheese, softened

⅓ cup fat-free Greek yogurt or light sour cream

⅓ cup grated Parmesan cheese

2 garlic cloves, crushed in press

¼ teaspoon salt

¼ teaspoon ground black pepper

1 package (9-ounce) frozen artichokes, thawed, patted dry, and chopped

1 lemon

snipped fresh chives, for garnish

1. Preheat oven to 400°F. Line large cookie sheet with foil. Cut bread in half lengthwise, then cut each piece in half across. With your hands, press bread to flatten.

2. Arrange bread, cut sides up, on prepared cookie sheet. Brush with oil and sprinkle with 1 cup mozzarella. Bake for 5 to 7 minutes or until cheese melts.

3. In large bowl, mix spinach, cream cheese, yogurt, Parmesan, garlic, salt, and pepper until blended. Remove bread from oven and divide cheese mixture among pieces of bread, spreading evenly. Top with artichokes and remaining ¼ cup mozzarella. Bake for 12 to 18 minutes longer or until golden brown.

4. Grate peel of half the lemon over pizzas. Garnish with chives.

EACH SERVING

Calories: About 645
Protein: 32G
Carbohydrates: 61G
Total Fat: 31G (Saturated Fat: 14G)
Fiber: 6G
Sodium: 1,245MG

Ham & Cheese Pizza

Prepare Spinach-Artichoke Pizza as directed through step 2. In small bowl, mix **3 tablespoons Dijon mustard, 3 tablespoons apricot jam,** and **¼ teaspoon black pepper.** Divide mixture among pieces of bread, spreading evenly. Top with **6 ounces thinly sliced deli ham** and **1 small Granny Smith apple,** thinly sliced. Sprinkle pizzas with **¾ cup shredded Gruyère cheese** and **2 teaspoons chopped fresh rosemary leaves.** Bake for 10 to 15 minutes or until golden brown. Serves 4.

EACH SERVING: About 590 Calories, 31G Protein, 66G Carbohydrate, 22G Total Fat (8G Saturated), 3G Fiber, 1,480MG Sodium

Cheeseburger Pizza

Prepare Spinach-Artichoke Pizza as directed through step 2. Spread **1 cup marinara sauce** on bread. Divide **8 ounces 90-percent-lean ground beef sirloin** among pieces of bread, distributing evenly. Sprinkle with **¼ teaspoon each salt and black pepper.** Top with **¾ cup shredded Cheddar cheese.** In small bowl, toss **½ small red onion,** finely chopped, and **1 teaspoon oil.** Sprinkle onion on pizzas. Bake for 15 to 20 minutes or until onion is tender and meat is cooked through. Serves 4.

EACH SERVING: About 620 Calories, 35G Protein, 55G Carbohydrate, 29G Total Fat (12G Saturated), 3G Fiber, 1,210MG Sodium

Thin-Crust
VEGGIE PIZZA

If you love an ultrathin crust, use a flour tortilla! The result is a super-crisp crust with zero sogginess. (Ditto for our variation recipes.)

ACTIVE TIME → 10 MINUTES TOTAL TIME → 25 MINUTES MAKES → 4 SERVINGS

INGREDIENTS

nonstick cooking spray
4 (8-inch) flour tortillas
4 cups baby spinach
1 medium red pepper, very thinly sliced
1 medium zucchini, very thinly sliced
2 teaspoons minced garlic
2 teaspoons olive oil
½ teaspoon salt
½ teaspoon ground black pepper
¾ cup marinara sauce
4 ounces goat cheese, crumbled
¼ cup finely grated Parmesan cheese
¼ cup fresh basil leaves

EACH SERVING

Calories: About 325
Protein: 14G
Carbohydrates: 36G
Total Fat: 14G
(Saturated Fat: 7G)
Fiber: 4G
Sodium: 1,165MG

1. Arrange oven racks in top and bottom thirds of oven. Preheat oven to 475°F. Spray 2 large cookie sheets with nonstick cooking spray; place 2 tortillas on each.

2. In large microwave-safe bowl, combine spinach, red pepper, zucchini, garlic, oil, salt, and black pepper; tossing to coat. Microwave uncovered on high for 2 minutes or until crisp-tender, stirring once. Drain, if necessary. Spread marinara sauce on tortillas. Top with vegetables and cheeses.

3. Bake for 12 minutes or until tortillas are crisp around edges, switching racks halfway through baking. When baked, take out of oven and top with basil.

SMART CHEF! Bump up the fiber in these recipes by using whole wheat tortillas.

→ BBQ Chicken Pizza

Prepare Thin-Crust Veggie Pizza as directed through step 1. In medium bowl, combine **2 cups chopped rotisserie chicken meat** and **½ cup barbecue sauce,** tossing to coat. Divide among tortillas. Top with **1 cup corn; ½ cup finely chopped red onion; 1 small orange pepper,** very thinly sliced; and **¾ cup shredded smoked mozzarella.** Bake as directed in step 3. Top with **¼ cup fresh cilantro,** chopped. Serves 4.

EACH SERVING: About 500 Calories, 34G Protein, 51G Carbohydrate, 18G Total Fat (8G Saturated), 3G Fiber, 1,370MG Sodium

→ Tex-Mex Pizza

Prepare Thin-Crust Veggie Pizza as directed through step 1. Combine **1 can (15 ounces) fat-free refried beans, ½ teaspoon chili powder,** and **¼ teaspoon ground cumin;** spread on tortillas. Top with **1 can (15 ounces) no-salt-added kidney beans,** rinsed; **1 cup shredded pepper Jack cheese;** and **1 avocado,** sliced. Bake as directed in step 3. Top with **1 cup chunky salsa** and **3 cups shredded romaine lettuce.** Serve with **lime wedges.** Serves 4.

EACH SERVING: About 650 Calories, 29G Protein, 67G Carbohydrate, 29G Total Fat (13G Saturated), 19G Fiber, 1,485MG Sodium

FUN FOOD!

Cheesy Monkey
BREAD

Monkey bread refers to a loaf made from pieces of yeast dough dipped in butter and baked in a pan. Sometimes called *bubble bread* or *pull-apart bread*, it's fun to serve because all your guests can use their fingers to help themselves.

ACTIVE TIME → 10 MINUTES   TOTAL TIME → 40 MINUTES (PLUS RISING)   MAKES → 10 SERVINGS

INGREDIENTS

2 batches Pizza-Tastic Dough, page 106

5 tablespoons butter

1 garlic clove, crushed with press

2 tablespoons dried onion flakes

1 tablespoon sesame seeds

2 green onions, finely chopped, plus 2 tablespoons finely chopped green onions

1 cup coarsely shredded Gruyère cheese

2 tablespoons finely chopped fresh parsley

1 cup marinara sauce, heated, for dipping

EACH SERVING

Calories: About 445
Protein: 12G
Carbohydrates: 64G
Total Fat: 15G
(Saturated Fat: 7G)
Fiber: 3G
Sodium: 707MG

1. Preheat oven to 400°F. Grease 10- to 12-cup Bundt pan and then dust with flour. On lightly floured surface, shape each ball of Pizza-Tastic Dough into 8-inch square.

2. In small microwave-safe bowl, combine 4 tablespoons butter and garlic. Cover with vented plastic wrap and microwave on high for 1 minute or until butter melts; brush generously onto dough. Sprinkle 1 square with onion flakes and sesame seeds. Sprinkle the other with 2 chopped green onions.

3. Cut each square into 1-inch pieces. Layer ⅓ of each flavored dough, buttered side down, onto bottom of prepared Bundt pan. Top with ½ cup Gruyère cheese; repeat with ⅓ of each dough and remaining ½ cup Gruyère cheese to make second layer. Top with remaining dough pieces. Melt remaining 1 tablespoon butter; brush on top of dough and sprinkle with remaining 2 tablespoons chopped green onions and parsley. Cover pan with clean kitchen towel and let rise in warm place for 20 minutes.

4. Bake bread for 25 to 30 minutes or until top is golden brown. Cool bread in pan for 5 minutes. Turn the bread over onto plate; remove pan. Serve warm with marinara sauce for dipping.

Moroccan
PIZZA

Pitas are perfect for pizza on the fly. Keep a stash of pitas in your freezer so
you can try all our variations. Just microwave each pita on high for 20 seconds to thaw;
then bake to a crispy, cracker-y crunch.

ACTIVE TIME → **15 MINUTES**   **TOTAL TIME** → **25 MINUTES**   **MAKES** → **4 SERVINGS**

INGREDIENTS

4 (5- to 6-inch) pitas

2 teaspoons olive oil

2 cups shredded rotisserie
chicken meat

1 cup marinara sauce

½ teaspoon ground cumin

¼ teaspoon ground
cinnamon

¼ teaspoon ground black
pepper

½ cup shredded carrots

¼ cup pitted green olives,
sliced

4 ounces (1 cup) shredded
part-skim mozzarella
cheese

2 green onions, sliced,
for garnish

EACH SERVING

Calories: About 430
Protein: 33G
Carbohydrates: 43G
Total Fat: 14G
(Saturated Fat: 5G)
Fiber: 4G
Sodium: 1,200MG

1. Preheat oven to 450°F. Line large cookie sheet with foil. Arrange pitas on prepared cookie sheet in single layer; brush pitas with oil.

2. In large bowl, combine chicken, marinara sauce, cumin, cinnamon, and pepper until evenly coated. Divide among pitas. Top evenly with carrots, olives, and mozzarella.

3. Bake for 10 to 15 minutes or until cheese is melted and pitas are crisp around edges. Garnish with green onions.

SMART CHEF! For fun party snacks, prepare this recipe using mini pitas that are cut into quarters after they've been baked. Your friends will love these adorable mini pizza slices!

→ Hawaiian Pizza

Prepare Moroccan Pizza as directed through step 1. Spread **1 cup marinara sauce** on pitas. Top with **1½ cups shredded pepper Jack or Monterey Jack cheese**; **4 ounces ham**, chopped; and **1 cup pineapple chunks**, chopped. Bake for 12 to 15 minutes or until pitas are crisp around edges. Garnish with **chopped fresh parsley**. Serves 4.

EACH SERVING: About 450 Calories, 20G Protein, 47G Carbohydrate, 20G Total Fat (10G Saturated), 4G Fiber, 1,300MG Sodium

→ Cheesy Bacon-Broccoli Pizza

Prepare Moroccan Pizza as directed through step 1. Arrange **6 slices bacon** in single layer on large microwave-safe, paper towel–lined plate; microwave on high for 2 minutes. Transfer to cutting board and chop. In medium bowl, combine **1½ cups broccoli florets**, chopped; **1 teaspoon oil**; and **⅛ teaspoon salt**; tossing to coat. Sprinkle pitas with **2 cups shredded sharp Cheddar cheese**. Top with **1 large tomato**, seeded and chopped, and broccoli mixture; sprinkle with bacon. Bake for 12 to 15 minutes. Serves 4.

EACH SERVING: About 495 Calories, 23G Protein, 39G Carbohydrate, 28G Total Fat (14G Saturated), 3G Fiber, 970MG Sodium

FUN FOOD!

Cookie "PIZZA"

Any way you slice it, this "pizza" is serious fun. Top the entire pie with your favorite spread and toppings or use our suggested combos to create a different flavor for each wedge.

ACTIVE TIME → 10 MINUTES   TOTAL TIME → 30 MINUTES (PLUS COOKING)   MAKES → 8 SERVINGS

INGREDIENTS
nonstick cooking spray
1 tube (16.5 ounces) refrigerated sugar-cookie dough
¼ cup all-purpose flour
assorted spreads and toppings, below

1. Preheat oven to 350°F. Line large cookie sheet with foil and spray with nonstick cooking spray.

2. Knead flour into cookie dough until combined. With your hands, roll dough into ball, then pat dough into disk. Place disk in center of your prepared cookie sheet. With rolling pin, roll dough into 11-inch round. Bake for 20 to 25 minutes or until edges are golden brown.

3. While crust bakes, set out spreads and toppings. While "pizza" is still warm, use pizza cutter or large chef's knife to cut into 8 wedges. Cool pizza completely on wire rack. Add assorted spreads and toppings:

→ **Sunflower Seed Butter, Raspberries, Granola**

→ **Low-fat Vanilla Yogurt, Strawberries, Almonds**

→ **Hazelnut-Chocolate Spread, Mini Marshmallows**

→ **Raspberry Jam, Butterscotch Chips**

→ **Hazelnut-Chocolate Spread, Heart Sprinkles**

→ **Raspberry Jam, Pecans, Mini Chocolate Chips**

→ **Nut Butter, Bananas, Dried Cranberries**

→ **Low-fat Vanilla Yogurt, Toasted Coconut, Chocolate Shavings**

5

Holidays & Special Bakes

Nothing marks a special occasion like a home-baked treat—especially when you're the proud baker. Start a party with our easy appetizers (all use store-bought puff pastry) or make your valentine a to-die-for Chocolate Ganache Tart (it's gluten-free!). We've also got authentic Irish Soda Bread for St. Patty's Day, Candy Cottontail Cookies for Easter, and Pumpkin Patch Cakes for Halloween. To round out the collection, we offer a dozen easiest-ever Christmas cookies to choose from, plus a mile-high gingerbread cake. Make any of these scrumptious recipes, and you'll be the star of the celebration!

Party Bites!

Want to serve some fancy appetizers? Simple! Pick a recipe at left, grab a
(17.25-ounce) box of frozen puff pastry, then bake dozens of cheesy, flaky appetizers that
are sure to be the hit of the party. Each box contains two sheets of frozen dough. To use,
thaw the folded sheets at room temperature on paper towels until pliable. If you're
rolling the dough, use a lightly floured surface and rolling pin.

Sprigs in a Blanket

Preheat oven to 425°F. Line 1 or 2 large cookie sheets with parchment paper. Roll 1 pastry sheet into 10-inch square. Brush sheet with **3 tablespoons Dijon mustard**, sprinkle with ¼ **cup grated Pecorino cheese**, and line with **2 to 3 large slices very thinly sliced prosciutto**. With sharp knife or pizza cutter, cut sheet in half; then cut halves into twenty ½-inch-wide, 5-inch-long strips. Wrap each strip around **1 stalk asparagus**, prosciutto side facing in. Place on prepared cookie sheets. Lightly spray wrapped asparagus spears with **nonstick cooking spray**. Bake for 20 to 25 minutes or until golden. Makes 40.

EACH WRAPPED ASPARAGUS: About 35 Calories, 1G Protein, 3G Carbohydrate, 2G Total Fat (1G Saturated), 0G Fiber, 82MG Sodium

Spanakopita

Preheat oven to 400°F. Line 15½ x 10½-inch rimmed baking sheet with parchment paper. Mix **3 packages (10 ounces each) frozen chopped spinach**, thawed and squeezed dry; **8 ounces crumbled feta cheese; 2 large eggs**, beaten; **2 green onions**, chopped; and ¼ **teaspoon each salt and black pepper**. Roll 2 pastry sheets into 15 x 10-inch rectangles; place 1 sheet on prepared baking sheet. Top with spinach mixture, leaving a border. Top with remaining pastry sheet; press to seal. Brush top with **1 large egg**, beaten. Bake for 25 minutes or until golden brown. Cool in pan on wire rack. Cut into 3-inch squares, then triangles. Makes 30 triangles.

EACH TRIANGLE: About 105 Calories, 4G Protein, 7G Carbohydrate, 7G Total Fat (2G Saturated), 1G Fiber, 196MG Sodium

Brie en Croûte

Preheat oven to 400°F. Line 15½ x 10½-inch rimmed baking sheet with parchment paper. Combine ⅓ **cup dried cranberries, 2 tablespoons cran-raspberry juice**, ½ **teaspoon grated lemon peel**, and ¼ **teaspoon salt**. Cut 1 pastry sheet into 6 x 9-inch rectangle, and place on prepared baking sheet. Roll into 14-inch square; place **1 wheel (1 pound) Brie cheese** in center. Cut off top rind of Brie; discard. Top with cranberry mixture. Gather pastry around Brie; twist in center. Secure twist with kitchen string; trim excess dough. Bake for 25 minutes or golden brown. Serves 12.

EACH SERVING: About 225 Calories, 9G Protein, 11G Carbohydrate, 16G Total Fat (8G Saturated), 0G Fiber, 386MG Sodium

Gluten-Free
CHOCOLATE GANACHE TART

This gorgeous tart is perfect for Valentine's Day. You can also garnish the top with raspberries to give the cake an overall brighter look.

ACTIVE TIME → **15 MINUTES**   **TOTAL TIME** → **25 MINUTES** (PLUS COOLING AND CHILLING)   **MAKES** → **8 SERVINGS**

INGREDIENTS

1 cup shredded sweetened coconut

1 cup salted gluten-free pretzels, crushed into small pieces

½ cup rice flour

½ cup coconut oil, melted

3 tablespoons brown sugar

2 tablespoons unsweetened cocoa

1 cup coconut milk

6 ounces dark chocolate, finely chopped

pinch salt

pomegranate seeds, for garnish, optional

EACH SERVING

Calories: About 445
Protein: 4G
Carbohydrates: 37G
Total Fat: 33G
(Saturated Fat: 26G)
Fiber: 4G
Sodium: 200MG

1. Preheat oven to 375°F. Grease 9-inch tart pan with removable bottom.

2. In large bowl, combine shredded coconut, pretzels, rice flour, melted coconut oil, sugar, and cocoa. Transfer to prepared tart pan. With your hands, firmly press mixture into bottom and up side of pan in even layer; place on cookie sheet. Bake for 10 minutes. Cool crust completely on wire rack.

3. In small saucepan, heat coconut milk over medium heat until just bubbling at edges, whisking occasionally. Place chocolate and salt in medium heatproof bowl. Pour hot coconut milk over chocolate. Let stand for 5 minutes. Gently whisk until smooth. Pour into tart shell. Refrigerate, uncovered, for 2 hours or until set. Once set, tart can be made ahead, covered with plastic wrap, for up to 2 days. To serve, garnish with pomegranate seeds, if using.

SMART CHEF! If the chocolate is more than 70 percent cacao, add 2 tablespoons brown sugar with chocolate and salt in step 3.

Irish Soda
BREAD

Flavored with currants and caraway seeds, this St. Patrick's Day treat is *fragrant* (meaning it has a distinctive aroma and taste) and surprisingly simple to make.

ACTIVE TIME → **15 MINUTES**   **TOTAL TIME** → **1 HOUR 15 MINUTES** (PLUS COOLING)   **MAKES** → **12 SERVINGS**

INGREDIENTS

4 cups all-purpose flour
¼ cup sugar
1 tablespoon baking
  powder
1½ teaspoons salt
1 teaspoon baking soda
6 tablespoons butter
1 cup dried currants
2 teaspoons caraway seeds
1½ cups low-fat buttermilk

EACH SERVING

Calories: About 270
Protein: 6G
Carbohydrates: 47G
Total Fat: 7G
(Saturated Fat: 4G)
Fiber: 2G
Sodium: 639MG

1. Preheat oven to 350°F. Grease large cookie sheet.

2. In large bowl with wire whisk, mix flour, sugar, baking powder, salt, and baking soda. With pastry blender or 2 knives used scissors-fashion, cut in butter until mixture resembles coarse crumbs. Stir in currants and caraway seeds, then buttermilk, until flour is moistened.

3. Turn dough onto well-floured surface; knead dough 8 to 10 times, just until combined. Shape into flattened ball; transfer to prepared cookie sheet. Cut ¼-inch-deep *X* into top using a knife.

4. Bake 1 hour or until toothpick inserted in center of loaf comes out clean. Cool loaf completely on wire rack.

Classic
MANDELBROT

Mandelbrot, or "almond bread," is a favorite Jewish cookie that resembles Italian biscotti, but the slices are not baked quite as crisp.

ACTIVE TIME → 30 MINUTES   **TOTAL TIME** → 1 HOUR 10 MINUTES (PLUS COOLING)   **MAKES** → 4 DOZEN COOKIES

INGREDIENTS

3¾ cups all-purpose flour

2 teaspoons baking powder

½ teaspoon salt

3 large eggs

1 cup sugar

¾ cup vegetable oil

2 teaspoons vanilla extract

¼ teaspoon almond extract

1 teaspoon freshly grated orange peel

1 cup slivered blanched almonds, toasted and coarsely chopped

EACH COOKIE

Calories: About 105

Protein: 2G

Carbohydrates: 12G

Total Fat: 5G

(Saturated Fat: 1G)

Fiber: 1G

Sodium: 50MG

1. Preheat oven to 350°F. In large bowl with wire whisk, mix flour, baking powder, and salt.

2. In large bowl with mixer on medium speed, beat eggs and sugar until light lemon-colored. Add oil, extracts, and orange peel, and beat until blended. With wooden spoon, beat in flour mixture until combined. Stir in almonds.

3. Divide dough in half. On large ungreased cookie sheet, drop each half of dough by spoonfuls down length of cookie sheet. With lightly floured hands, shape each half of dough into 12-inch-long log, 4 inches apart (dough will be slightly sticky). Bake for 30 minutes or until dough is light-colored and firm. Cool logs on cookie sheet on wire rack for 10 minutes or until easy to handle. Arrange oven racks in top and bottom thirds of oven.

4. Transfer logs to cutting board. With serrated knife, cut each log crosswise into ½-inch-thick slices. Place slices, cut side down, on 2 ungreased cookie sheets. Bake for 7 to 8 minutes or until golden, rotating cookie sheets between upper and lower racks halfway through baking. With metal spatula, transfer cookies to wire racks to cool completely.

Spring Greens & MATZO FRITTATA

Matzo is an unleavened bread that is eaten during the Jewish holiday of Passover.
If you've got leftover matzo, this tasty bake with asparagus and peas will put them to good use.

ACTIVE TIME → 10 MINUTES TOTAL TIME → 50 MINUTES (PLUS COOLING) MAKES → 6 SERVINGS

INGREDIENTS

nonstick cooking spray

1 tablespoon butter

1 bunch (about 1 pound) thin asparagus, trimmed and cut into 1-inch lengths

5 sheets matzo, broken into large chunks

5 large eggs

1 cup fresh basil leaves, chopped

1 cup frozen peas, thawed

1 tablespoon freshly grated lemon peel

1 teaspoon salt

½ teaspoon ground black pepper

EACH SERVING

Calories: About 200
Protein: 10G
Carbohydrates: 25G
Total Fat: 6G
(Saturated Fat: 3G)
Fiber: 3G
Sodium: 465MG

1. Preheat oven to 350°F. Spray 8 x 8-inch baking dish with nonstick cooking spray.

2. In 12-inch skillet over medium heat, melt butter. Add asparagus and cook for 5 to 8 minutes or until crisp-tender. Remove skillet from heat and cool.

3. Meanwhile, in medium bowl, pour 1 cup warm water over matzo. Let stand for 5 minutes or until softened. Drain.

4. In large bowl with wire whisk, beat eggs. Stir in asparagus, matzo, basil, peas, lemon peel, salt, and pepper. Pour into prepared baking dish. Bake for 40 minutes or until top is golden brown and center is set. Cooled frittata may be made ahead, covered with plastic wrap, and refrigerated for up to 3 days.

Pumpkin PATCH CAKES

Make these cakes for your next Halloween party, and it'll be a spook-tacular occasion.

TOTAL TIME → 1 HOUR (PLUS COOLING AND STANDING)   **MAKES → 6 CAKES**

INGREDIENTS

nonstick cooking spray

1 (15.25-ounce) box yellow or chocolate cake mix

orange and green gel food coloring

2 cups confectioners' sugar

orange and green crystal sugar or candy decorations

pretzel rods or sticks

marzipan, for leaves

EACH ½ CAKE WITHOUT DECORATIONS

Calories: About 340
Protein: 3G
Carbohydrates: 51G
Total Fat: 14G
(Saturated Fat: 2G)
Fiber: 0G
Sodium: 258MG

1. Preheat oven to 350°F. Spray 12 mini Bundt pans with nonstick cooking spray.

2. Prepare cake mix (tint with food coloring, if desired) and bake as directed, filling pans halfway with batter.

3. When cakes are done, unmold them onto wire rack and cool completely.

4. In 4-cup measuring cup, mix confectioners' sugar and 3 to 4 tablespoons water to make thick glaze. With sharp knife, trim bottom of each cake flat; assemble into pairs. Using a small amount of glaze drizzled on flat sides of cakes, attach pairs to form 6 pumpkins.

5. Drizzle pumpkin cakes with glaze and/or sprinkle with crystal sugar or candy decorations. Break pretzel rods to fit as stems. Moisten pretzels with water and roll in crystal sugar. Insert into centers of pumpkins.

6. Tint marzipan with green food coloring for leaves. Roll and cut as desired and place around pretzel stems. Let cakes stand until glaze is set.

SMART CHEF! If you want, try melted apricot jam instead of the glaze to sandwich the cakes together. It'll save you some time!

Sweet & Salted
CARAMEL NUT PIE

If you want to try something different than typical pecan pie for Thanksgiving, this recipe is the way to go. It has all the yummy, nutty flavor of pecans—plus that of walnuts and hazelnuts!

ACTIVE TIME ➜ 30 MINUTES   TOTAL TIME ➜ 1 HOUR 10 MINUTES (PLUS COOLING)   MAKES ➜ 12 SERVINGS

INGREDIENTS

1 refrigerated ready-to-use piecrust (for a 9-inch pie), softened as label directs

4 cups mixed unsalted pecans, walnuts, and hazelnuts, toasted

1½ cups sugar

3 tablespoons light corn syrup

6 tablespoons unsalted butter, cut into small pieces

½ teaspoon kosher salt

1 cup heavy cream

flaked sea salt, optional

EACH SERVING

Calories: About 520
Protein: 8G
Carbohydrates: 50G
Total Fat: 36G
(Saturated Fat: 12G)
Fiber: 3G
Sodium: 158MG

1. Heat oven to 375°F. Line 9-inch pie plate with piecrust. Gently press dough against bottom and up side of plate without stretching it. Tuck overhang under and crimp to form raised edge.

2. Line crust with nonstick foil; fill with pie weights or dried beans. Bake for 15 minutes. Remove parchment and weights. Bake for 5 to 10 minutes longer or until pastry just starts to turn golden. Transfer crust to wire rack; spread nuts in crust.

3. Reduce oven temperature to 350°F. In heavy-bottomed medium saucepan, place sugar, ½ cup water, and corn syrup. Without stirring, cook over medium-high heat for about 1 minute or until bubbles begin to form at edges, swirling pan occasionally. Bring to a simmer, then increase heat to high and boil for 6 to 10 minutes or until mixture is a rich caramel color, swirling pan occasionally. Immediately remove pan from heat, add butter and kosher salt, and swirl pan until butter melts.

4. Return pan to medium heat, add cream (it will bubble up), and whisk for about 1 minute or until smooth, slightly thickened, and a deep amber color. Pour caramel over nuts; place pie in oven. Bake for 10 to 15 minutes or until filling is gently bubbling.

5. Cool pie completely on wire rack. Sprinkle with flaked sea salt, if using.

Original Pumpkin Pie
WITH MAPLE WHIP

It wouldn't be Thanksgiving without pumpkin pie for dessert.
Our recipe includes a dollop of maple whipped cream on every slice.

ACTIVE TIME → 15 MINUTES   **TOTAL TIME** → 1 HOUR 30 MINUTES (PLUS STANDING AND COOLING)   **MAKES** → 12 SERVINGS

INGREDIENTS

1 refrigerated ready-to-use piecrust (for a 9-inch pie), softened as label directs

3 large eggs

¼ cup packed light brown sugar

1 (15-ounce) can pure pumpkin

½ cup whole milk

1 teaspoon vanilla extract

¾ teaspoon ground cinnamon

¾ teaspoon ground ginger

½ cup plus 6 tablespoons pure maple syrup

1 cup heavy cream

¼ teaspoon kosher salt

EACH SERVING

Calories: About 260
Protein: 3G
Carbohydrates: 33G
Total Fat: 13G
(Saturated Fat: 7G)
Fiber: 0G
Sodium: 141MG

1. Heat oven to 350°F. Line 9-inch pie plate with piecrust. Gently press dough against bottom and up side of pie plate without stretching it. Tuck overhang under and crimp to form raised edge. Refrigerate until ready to fill.

2. In large bowl with wire whisk, beat eggs, brown sugar, pumpkin, milk, vanilla, cinnamon, ginger, ½ cup maple syrup, ¼ cup cream, and salt until combined.

3. Pour pumpkin mixture into prepared pie shell. Bake for 60 to 65 minutes or until edge of filling is just set but center still jiggles slightly and crust is golden brown. Cool pie on wire rack to room temperature.

4. About 10 minutes before serving, in large bowl with mixer on medium-high speed, beat remaining ¾ cup cream and remaining 6 tablespoons maple syrup until soft peaks form. Serve with pie.

Extra-Easy
CHRISTMAS CUTOUT COOKIES

Pressed for time, but still want to do holiday baking? In just 15 minutes, you can turn cookie dough into decadent Christmas cookies. All you need is a roll of refrigerated sugar-cookie dough, some flour, and a little hands-on action.

Add Flour: Break **1 tube (16.5 ounces) sugar-cookie dough** into pieces. On a floured board, knead in **½ cup all-purpose flour**, a little at a time, working dough until smooth. Don't be afraid to put some muscle into it.

Roll and Cut: Form dough into a disk. Lightly flour the rolling pin and your work surface, then roll the dough to ¼-inch thickness. Cut out cookies (simple shapes work best). Reroll the scraps and repeat.

Dress 'Em Up: Transfer your cutouts to a large cookie sheet. For the easiest decorations ever, sprinkle them (use a teaspoon or your fingers) with **colored or clear sparkly sugar crystals**.

Chill, Then Bake: Freeze the cookies on their sheet for at least 30 minutes (it helps keep their shape), then bake as the label directs. We like the flavor better when the cookies get a little browner.

FUN FOOD!

Vanilla
SUGAR DOUGH

I'll bet you didn't know that cookie dough could be used in so many ways!
For all you vanilla-lovers out there, this is the recipe for you!

ACTIVE TIME → **30 MINUTES**   **TOTAL TIME** → **1 HOUR 10 MINUTES** (PLUS CHILLING)   **MAKES** → **ABOUT 3 DOZEN COOKIES**

INGREDIENTS

3 cups all-purpose flour
¾ teaspoon baking powder
½ teaspoon salt
1 cup (2 sticks) butter, softened
1 cup sugar
1 large egg
2 teaspoons vanilla extract
1 teaspoon almond extract

EACH COOKIE

Calories: About 110
Protein: 1G
Carbohydrates: 14G
Total Fat: 5G
(Saturated Fat: 3G)
Fiber: 0G
Sodium: 87MG

1. Preheat oven to 375°F.

2. In large bowl with wire whisk, mix flour, baking powder, and salt. In another large bowl with mixer on medium-high speed, beat butter and sugar until smooth. Beat in egg, then extracts, occasionally scraping bowl with rubber spatula. Reduce speed to low; gradually beat in flour mixture just until blended.

3. Divide dough into 4 equal pieces; flatten each into a disk. Wrap each disk tightly in plastic wrap and refrigerate for 30 minutes or until dough is firm but not hard. For cutouts: Remove 1 disk of dough from refrigerator. On one half of lightly floured large sheet parchment paper, with floured rolling pin, roll dough ⅛ inch thick. With floured cookie cutter, cut out shapes. With paring knife or small metal spatula, remove dough between cutouts. On other half of parchment, reroll the scraps of dough and cut out more shapes.

4. Slide parchment onto large cookie sheet. Bake for 10 to 12 minutes or until edges are golden. With spatula, transfer cookies to wire racks to cool completely. Repeat with remaining dough.

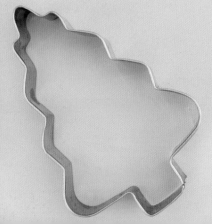

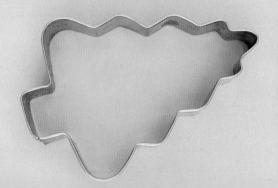

Choco-Dipped Trees

Roll out Vanilla Sugar Dough to ⅛ inch thickness. Cut into tree shapes and bake according to recipe directions. When cool, dip half of each tree in **melted dark chocolate** and sprinkle with **multicolored sugar crystals**.

Thumbprint Jammers

Instead of cutting Vanilla Sugar Dough, scoop into 1-inch balls and roll each in bowl of **small, silver nonpareils**; place on parchment-lined cookie sheet. Make indentations by pressing your thumb into centers. Bake according to recipe directions. When cool, fill centers with **jam**.

Crunchy Candy Canes

Roll out Vanilla Sugar Dough to ⅛ inch thickness. Cut into candy cane shapes and bake according to recipe directions. When cool, drizzle with **melted white chocolate** and sprinkle with **crushed peppermints**.

Hanukkah Squares

Roll out Vanilla Sugar Dough to ⅛ inch thickness. Cut into squares. Bake according to recipe directions. When cool, brush stripes of **Decorator's Icing**, page 146, on 2 edges. Dip one edge into bowl of **blue sugar crystals** and other edge into bowl of **white sugar crystals**.

WINTER
SPICE DOUGH

It wouldn't be the holidays without a little spice. Prepare **Vanilla Sugar Dough**, page 144, as directed, but whisk **1 teaspoon ground cinnamon**, **½ teaspoon ground ginger**, and **¼ teaspoon ground cloves** into flour mixture. Beat **2 tablespoons molasses** into dough with egg in step 2.

HOW TO: DECORATOR'S ICING

In large bowl with mixer on medium speed, beat **1 package (16 ounces) confectioners' sugar**, **3 tablespoons meringue powder**, and ⅓ cup warm water for 5 minutes or until blended and mixture is very stiff. Makes about 3 cups. Separate into bowls and add drops of various food colorings to make different colors, stirring to combine.

EACH TABLESPOON: About 40 Calories, 0G Protein, 10G Carbohydrate, 0G Total Fat (0G Saturated), 0G Fiber, 3MG Sodium

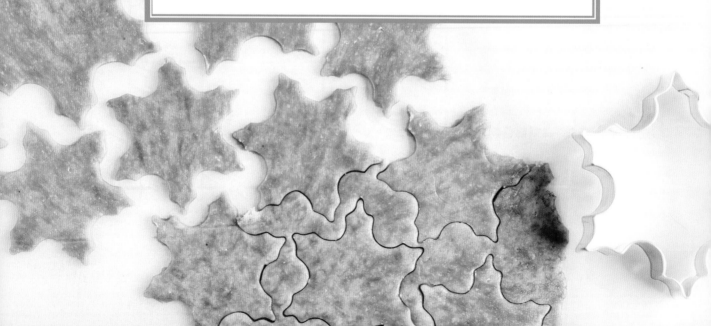

Sprinkle Mittens

Roll out Winter Spice Dough to ⅛ inch thickness. Cut into mitten shapes. Bake according to Vanilla Sugar Dough recipe directions, page 144. When cool, decorate with **Decorator's Icing, colored sprinkles,** and **mini marshmallows.**

Nutty Snowballs

Instead of cutting Winter Spice Dough, scoop into 1-inch balls. Roll each dough ball in bowl of **finely chopped pecans.** Place nut-covered dough balls on parchment-lined cookie sheet. Pat to flatten. Bake according to Vanilla Sugar Dough recipe directions, page 144. Dust with **confectioners' sugar.**

Glazed "Waffle" Cookies

Roll out Winter Spice Dough to ⅛ inch thickness. Cut into rounds. With potato masher, gently press dough to form a pattern before baking. Bake according to Vanilla Sugar Dough recipe directions, page 144. When cool, paint a pattern with **Decorator's Icing.**

Cranberry-Pistachio Wreaths

Roll out Winter Spice Dough to ⅛ inch thickness. Cut into wreath shapes. Bake according to Vanilla Sugar Dough recipe directions, page 144. When cool, decorate with **Decorator's Icing, finely chopped dried cranberries,** and **pistachios.**

147

Chocolate
TRUFFLE DOUGH

Chocolate lovers, get your tastebuds ready! Prepare Vanilla Sugar Dough, page 144, as directed, but replace ½ cup flour with **½ cup unsweetened cocoa**. Beat **2 ounces semisweet chocolate**, melted and cooled slightly, into dough with egg in Step 2.

HOW TO: COOKIE ART

Follow these tips to decorate like a pro:

- Tint Decorator's Icing, page 146 with food coloring as desired; press plastic wrap directly onto the surface to keep it from drying out.

- For piping, thin icing slightly with water. Spoon into piping bags with small writing tips to decorate cooled cookies.

- For a spreadable glaze to cover larger areas, add warm water to thin icing to the texture of sour cream.

- Pipe your icing border first to keep the glaze from escaping.

- Use a toothpick to drag the glaze to join the outline.

- Add sprinkles and other decorations while the icing/glaze is wet. Let it dry before serving.

Cocoa-Peppermint Buttons

Roll out Chocolate Truffle Dough to ⅛ inch thickness. Instead of cutting, scoop and roll dough into 1-inch balls; place dough balls on a parchment-lined cookie sheet. Pat to flatten. Bake according to Vanilla Sugar Dough recipe directions, page 144. After removing cookies from oven, immediately press **starlight mint** into center of each one.

Frosted Snowmen

Roll out Chocolate Truffle Dough to ⅛ inch thickness. Cut into snowman shapes. Bake according to Vanilla Sugar Dough recipe directions, page 144. When cool, decorate with **Decorator's Icing**, page 146, and **mini M&M's**.

Holly with Berries

Roll out Chocolate Truffle Dough to ⅛ inch thickness. Cut into holly leaf shapes. Bake according to Vanilla Sugar Dough recipe directions, page 144. When cool, decorate with **Decorator's Icing**, page 146, and **mini M&M's**.

Choco "Pretzels"

Instead of cutting Chocolate Truffle Dough, scoop and roll into ⅜ x 8-inch logs; twist into pretzel shapes. Bake according to Vanilla Sugar Dough recipe directions, page 144. When cool, drizzle with **Decorator's Icing**, page 146, and sprinkle with **white sugar crystals**.

Candy
COTTONTAIL COOKIES

Hop to it and bake a batch of these cute cookies in time for Easter Sunday or for your neighborhood Easter egg hunt. You can find cookie cutters at any kitchen supply store.

TOTAL TIME → 1 HOUR 15 MINUTES (PLUS COOLING AND STANDING)   **MAKES → 3 DOZEN COOKIES**

INGREDIENTS

Vanilla Sugar Cookie
   Dough, page 144
red food coloring
2 cans (16 ounces each)
   vanilla frosting
mini marshmallows
pink M&M's
pink candy-coated
   sunflower seeds

EACH FROSTED COOKIE
WITHOUT DECORATIONS

Calories: About 215
Protein: 1G
Carbohydrates: 31G
Total Fat: 9G
(Saturated Fat: 4G)
Fiber: 0G
Sodium: 133MG

1. Prepare Vanilla Sugar Cookie Dough as directed for cutouts (see page 144). With floured 3-inch-round cutter, cut out rounds for bodies. With floured 1-inch, egg-shaped cutter, cut out ovals for feet. Bake as directed.

2. With red food coloring, tint 1 can of frosting pink.

3. To assemble, spread white and pink frosting on cooled cookie rounds and ovals. Press ovals into edges of rounds; press marshmallows into centers for tails. Place M&M's in middle of feet and candy-coated sunflower seeds on edges of feet for toes. Let cookies stand for about 2 hours or until frosting is set.

Best-Ever
GINGERBREAD CAKE

This spiced cake is topped with a mound of whipped cream
and a snowlike dusting of confectioners' sugar. It's the perfect wintertime treat!

ACTIVE TIME → 20 MINUTES   **TOTAL TIME** → 1 HOUR 5 MINUTES (PLUS CHILLING AND COOLING)   **MAKES** → 12 SERVINGS

INGREDIENTS

3 cups all-purpose flour
2 teaspoons ground ginger
1 teaspoon baking soda
1 teaspoon ground cinnamon
½ teaspoon ground allspice
½ teaspoon ground nutmeg
½ teaspoon salt
¼ teaspoon ground cloves
¼ teaspoon ground black pepper
¾ cup (1½ sticks) butter, softened
1½ cups granulated sugar
1 teaspoon vanilla extract
2 large eggs
1 cup light (mild) molasses
whipped cream and confectioners' sugar, for garnish

EACH SERVING WITHOUT GARNISH

Calories: About 395
Protein: 5G
Carbohydrates: 68G
Total Fat: 13G
(Saturated Fat: 8G)
Fiber: 1G
Sodium: 305MG

1. Preheat oven to 350°F. Grease and flour a 9-inch springform pan.

2. In medium bowl with wire whisk, mix flour, ginger, baking soda, cinnamon, allspice, nutmeg, salt, cloves, and pepper.

3. In large bowl with mixer on medium-high speed, beat butter, granulated sugar, and vanilla for 3 minutes or until creamy, occasionally scraping down side of bowl with rubber spatula. Reduce speed to medium; add eggs, 1 at a time, beating well after each addition.

4. In 4-cup measuring cup or medium bowl, stir molasses into 1 cup very hot water. Reduce mixer speed to low. Alternately add flour mixture and molasses, beginning and ending with flour mixture, just until blended.

5. Pour batter into prepared springform pan; firmly tap pan against counter to release any bubbles. Bake for 45 to 55 minutes or until toothpick inserted in center of cake comes out clean. Cool cake, in pan, on wire rack for 15 minutes. With small metal spatula or knife, loosen edges and remove springform ring. Cool completely. Cake can be made ahead, wrapped in double layer of plastic wrap, then foil, and frozen for up to 1 month. Thaw in refrigerator.

6. To serve, top cake with whipped cream and dust with confectioners' sugar.

INDEX

PHOTO CREDITS

METRIC CONVERSION CHARTS

The recipes that appear in this cookbook use the standard United States method for measuring liquid and dry or solid ingredients (teaspoons, tablespoons, and cups). The information on this chart is provided to help cooks outside the U.S. successfully use these recipes. All equivalents are approximate.

METRIC EQUIVALENTS FOR DIFFERENT TYPES OF INGREDIENTS

STANDARD CUP	FINE POWDER (e.g. flour)	GRAIN (e.g. rice)	GRANULAR (e.g. sugar)	LIQUID SOLIDS (e.g. butter)	LIQUID (e.g. milk)
¾	105 g	113 g	143 g	150 g	180 ml
⅔	93 g	100 g	125 g	133 g	160 ml
½	70 g	75 g	95 g	100 g	120 ml
⅓	47 g	50 g	63 g	67 g	80 ml
¼	35 g	38 g	48 g	50 g	60 ml
⅛	18 g	19 g	24 g	25 g	30 ml

USEFUL EQUIVALENTS FOR LIQUID INGREDIENTS BY VOLUME

¼ tsp	=						1 ml
½ tsp	=						2 ml
1 tsp	=						5 ml
3 tsp	=	1 Tbsp	=		½ fl oz	=	15 ml
		2 Tbsp	=	⅛ cup	1 fl oz	=	30 ml
		4 Tbsp	=	¼ cup	2 fl oz	=	60 ml
		5⅓ Tbsp	=	⅓ cup	3 fl oz	=	80 ml
		8 Tbsp	=	½ cup	4 fl oz	=	120 ml
		10⅔ Tbsp	=	⅔ cup	5 fl oz	=	160 ml
		12 Tbsp	=	¾ cup	6 fl oz	=	180 ml
		16 Tbsp	=	1 cup	8 fl oz	=	240 ml
		1 pt	=	2 cups	16 fl oz	=	480 ml
		1 qt	=	4 cups	32 fl oz	=	960 ml
					33 fl oz	=	1000 ml = 1 L

USEFUL EQUIVALENTS FOR DRY INGREDIENTS BY WEIGHT

(To convert ounces to grams, multiply the number of ounces by 30.)

1 oz	=	¹⁄₁₆ lb	=	30 g
4 oz	=	¼ lb	=	120 g
8 oz	=	½ lb	=	240 g
12 oz	=	¾ lb	=	360 g
16 oz	=	1 lb	=	480 g

USEFUL EQUIVALENTS FOR COOKING/OVEN TEMPERATURES

	Fahrenheit	Celsius	Gas Mark
Freeze Water	32° F	0° C	
Room Temperature	68° F	20° C	
Boil Water	212° F	100° C	
Bake	325° F	160° C	3
	350° F	180° C	4
	375° F	190° C	5
	400° F	200° C	6
	425° F	220° C	7
	450° F	230° C	8
Broil			Grill

USEFUL EQUIVALENTS LENGTH

(To convert inches to centimeters, multiply the number of inches by 2.5.)

1 in	=				2.5 cm		
6 in	=	½ ft	=		15 cm		
12 in	=	1 ft	=		30 cm		
36 in	=	3 ft	=	1 yd	90 cm		
40 in	=				100 cm	=	1 m

GOOD HOUSEKEEPING
TRIPLE TEST PROMISE

At *Good Housekeeping*, we want to make sure that every recipe we print works in any oven, with any brand of ingredient, no matter what. That's why, in our test kitchens at the Good Housekeeping Research Institute, we go all out: We test each recipe at least three times—and, often, several more times after that.

When a recipe is first developed, one member of our team prepares the dish, and we judge it on these criteria: It must be delicious, family-friendly, healthful, and easy to make.

1 The recipe is then tested several more times to fine-tune the flavor and ease of preparation, always by the same team member, using the same equipment.

2 Next, another team member follows the recipe as written, varying the brands of ingredients and kinds of equipment. Even the types of stoves we use are changed.

3 A third team member repeats the whole process using yet another set of equipment and alternative ingredients. By the time the recipes appear on these pages, they are guaranteed to work in any kitchen, including yours. We promise.

HEARST BOOKS

An Imprint of Sterling Publishing Co., Inc.
1166 Avenue of the Americas
New York, NY 10036

ISBN 978-1-61837-269-7

The Good Housekeeping Cookbook Seal guarantees that the recipes in this cookbook meet the strict standards
of the Good Housekeeping Research Institute. The Institute has been a source of reliable information and a consumer advocate since
1900, and established its seal of approval in 1909. Every recipe has been triple-tested for ease, reliability, and great taste.

Hearst Communications, Inc., has made every effort to ensure that all information in this publication is accurate. However,
due to differing conditions, tools, and individual skills, Hearst Communications, Inc., cannot be responsible for any injuries, losses,
and/or damages that may result from the use of any information in this publication.

Distributed in Canada by Sterling Publishing
c/o Canadian Manda Group, 664 Annette Street
Toronto, Ontario M6S 2C8, Canada
Distributed in Australia by NewSouth Books
45 Beach Street, Coogee, NSW 2034, Australia

For information about custom editions, special sales, and premium and corporate purchases, please contact
Sterling Special Sales at 800-805-5489 or specialsales@sterlingpublishing.com.

Manufactured in China

Lot#:
2 4 6 8 10 9 7 5 3 1
07/18

goodhousekeeping.com
sterlingpublishing.com

Cover and interior design by Heather Kelly
For photo credits, see page 156